Easy
KITCHEN
SOLUTIONS

IKEA

CONTENTS

Cabinetcraft Kitchens

EDITORIAL
Series editor: Sheridan Carter
Managing editor: Susan Tomnay
Editorial coordinator: Margaret Kelly
UK editorial consultants: How-To Publications

CONTRIBUTORS
Leta Keens (The kitchen plan, Kitchen styles, The right floor, Colour and decor, Work surfaces, Kitchen outlook, Rubbish and fume disposal, Cleaning the kitchen)
Jane Sheard (Cooking in a good light, Sinks and taps, Bringing the outdoors in, Heating and cooling, Storage solutions, Appliances, Kids in the kitchen, The kitchen office, Safety in the kitchen)

PROJECT CONTRIBUTORS
Leigh Adams (Toolkit, Project 7)
Greg Slater (Project 1)
Greg Cheetham (Projects 2 and 6)
Mary-Anne Danaher (Project 3)
Colin Try (Projects 4, 10 and 11)
Tonia Todman (Project 5)
Graeme Haron (Project 8)
Paul Urquhart (Project 9)
Project Consultant: Greg Slater

PHOTOGRAPHY
Styling and Picture Research: Mary-Anne Danaher

Photographer: Simon Kenny (except where otherwise credited)

DESIGN AND PRODUCTION
Manager: Nadia Sbisa
Design and layout: Margie Mulray
Finished art: Chris Hatcher

ILLUSTRATIONS
Rod Westblade

COVER
Design: Frank Pithers
Photography: Simon Kenny

PUBLISHER
Philippa Sandall

Published by J.B. Fairfax Press Pty Ltd,
80-82 McLachlan Avenue,
Rushcutters Bay NSW 2011

EASY KITCHEN SOLUTIONS
Includes Index
ISBN 1 86343 029 6

Formatted by J.B. Fairfax Press Pty Ltd
Output by Adtype, Sydney
Printed by Toppan Printing Co, Hong Kong

Distributed in the UK by
J.B. Fairfax Press Ltd,
9 Trinity Centre, Park Farm Estate,
Wellingborough, Northants, UK
Tel: (0933) 402330
Fax: (0933) 402234

Distributed in Australia by
Newsagents Direct Distributors and
Storewide Magazine Distributors,
150 Bourke Road, Alexandria
NSW 2015

Distributed Internationally by
T.B.Clarke (Overseas) Pty Ltd,
80 McLachlan Avenue,
Rushcutters Bay NSW 2011
Tel: (02) 360 7566
Fax: (02) 360 7445

New Zealand Agents
Medialine Holdings Ltd,
P O Box 100,
243 North Shore Mail Centre
Tel: (09) 443 0250
Fax: (09) 443 0249

All care has been taken to ensure the accuracy of the information in this book but no responsibility is accepted for any errors or omissions.

*R*oll on the weekend! A time to stop, put your feet up, enjoy a drink, close your eyes and ... sink into a deep sleep? Certainly not! Its time to dream up your next home improvement project!

Whether you're starting from scratch with a new kitchen, remodelling your existing kitchen or you just want to add a few shelves, Easy Kitchen Solutions *will show you just how to do it.*

We've got plans for five different kitchen shapes, examples of four different kitchen styles, information on lighting, floors, surfaces, storage and appliances. And there are colour and decorating ideas too.

The eleven step-by-step projects in the book range from making simple cafe curtains, which will take an hour or two, to installing a kit kitchen, which will keep you busy for a whole weekend or more. They're all rated according to degree of difficulty (see Key to Projects, page 4).

Making changes in your kitchen is an extremely rewarding task, especially if those changes make the preparation and serving of food simpler. Most changes can be done without spending lots of money as long as you're prepared to put in a little time and effort.

Be sure to make yourself aware of the noise pollution laws in your area. You don't want to break the law (or alienate your neighbours) by using a power drill at 6 o'clock on a Saturday morning, no matter how keen you are to get started.

When making any of the projects, remember the golden rule of carpentry: measure twice and cut once.

The weekend is the natural time to undertake projects – after all, most of us only have the weekends to do work around the home. It's amazing what you can achieve, so why not give it a go? Spend a working weekend or two with Easy Kitchen Solutions *– and then put your feet up!*

KEY TO PROJECTS

PROJECT RATINGS	
🔨	for beginners
🔨🔨	for average skills
🔨🔨🔨	for the experienced

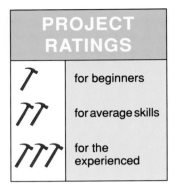

Project 1: Fold-down table (page 18)

🔨🔨

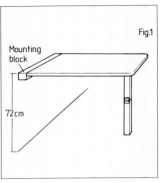

Project 2: Installing a kit kitchen (page 28)

🔨🔨🔨

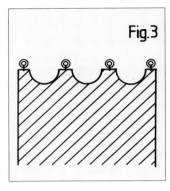

Project 3: Cafe curtains (page 33)

🔨

Project 4: Laying a vinyl tile floor (page 38)

🔨🔨

Project 5: Stencilling (page 46)

🔨

Project 6: Tiling a kitchen wall (page 51)

🔨🔨

Project 7: Cat door (page 53)

🔨🔨

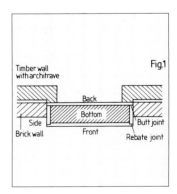

Project 8: Window box (page 57)

🔨🔨

Project 9: Making a kitchen garden (page 60)

🔨

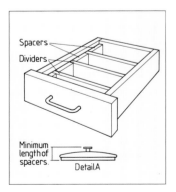

Project 10: Saucepan lid drawer (page 66)

🔨

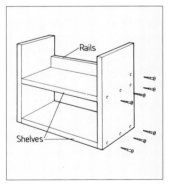

Project 10: Bookshelves (page 66)

🔨

Project 10: Plate rack (page 67)

Project 10: Wine rack (page 68)

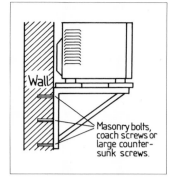

Project 10: Dresser shelves (page 68)

Project 11: Microwave shelf (page 72)

Wall

Masonry bolts, coach screws or large counter-sunk screws.

Tool Kit

Most of the projects require only basic tools, however an amateur carpenter will find that power tools not only make the job easier and quicker, but also much more accurate.

A basic tool kit consists of the following:

❏ **Hammer** A medium weight claw hammer with a wooden handle is probably the most versatile, but steel or fibreglass shanked hammers, although more expensive, will last longer.

❏ **Saw** A 10-point per 25 mm panel saw will be the best all-round unit, as it will cross cut and rip material of most general sizes.

❏ **Mitre box** Usually a simple wooden device which enables one to cut timber up to 125 mm wide at the exact angle desired, usually 90° or 45°. More sophisticated examples allow for wider cuts.

❏ **Chisels** These can be purchased individually, but are best bought in a set. Sets usually comprise three or more. A good starting set would consist of 13 mm, 19 mm and 25 mm chisels.

❏ **Screwdrivers** Like chisels these can be bought individually, but a set of five containing three widths of slotted and two

sizes of Phillips head (crosshead), would be a good starting kit.

❏ **Rule or tape** Probably the most important of all your tools. They are available in combination metric and imperial measurements.

❏ **Set square (try square)** Used to mark out and check material for square so that projects can be made accurately.

❏ **Smoothing plane** This traditional carpenter's tool is quite expensive but with care will last a lifetime. Instructions for its use and sharpening will normally come with it.

❏ **Knife** A utility knife is a very handy tool. Buy one with a retractable blade and use it carefully.

❏ **Cork block** This inexpensive piece of equipment is most useful when sandpapering.

❏ **Spirit level** Used for checking the vertical and horizontal planes, this is an essential tool

if cupboards, doors and kitchen worktops are on the job list.

❏ **Files** These are available in many shapes, lengths and grades. Best to start off with a 250 mm general purpose half-round file.

❏ **Pinch bar (crowbar)** A useful item to save your back, it can be used to lift heavy items and pull out large nails.

❏ **Pliers** 200 mm combination pliers will handle most jobs. Those with insulated handles are a good idea. There are big differences in the quality available and, like all tools, you get what you pay for.

❏ **Adjustable spanner** Buy a size suitable for your project, but 200 mm spanners handle most general work.

❏ **Clamps** These are your second pair of hands, used to hold timber, clamp joints etc. They come in various sizes and shapes and are commonly used in pairs. Two 200 mm G-clamps are the best to start off with.

❏ **Nail punch** Buy one small and one large for general purpose work.

❏ **Hacksaw** Ideal for cutting metal such as bolts, nails etc. Various tooth sizes are available.

❏ **Chalk line** A device that

automatically adds chalk to a length of string that can be stretched tight between two points then snapped against the surface where the line is required, leaving a well-defined line.

POWER TOOLS

❏ **Electric drill** A good all-round unit is a 10 mm 2-speed drill. Instructions are included in the box. A suitable accessory for the 240 volt drill is an extension cable of at least 5 m.

❏ **Electric screwdriver** Available in 240V and cordless versions. The cordless unit with a rechargeable battery is lightweight, easy to handle and ideal for awkward jobs.

❏ **Circular saw** This is a dangerous tool if not handled correctly, but with care it will cut solid timber and sheet material with ease. All power tools come with instructions from the manufacturer and these should be read carefully before use.

❏ **Jigsaw** Ideal for curved work and for cutting holes. Jigsaw blades are available in many grades for cutting wood, plastic and metal.

❏ **Sander** Two types are available – orbital and belt. Both types can use different types of abrasive paper to level off and smooth. They can be used for stripping paintwork, but both will leave score marks on the job, so a light rub with hand-held paper is required before painting or oiling.

❏ **Grinder** There are two types of grinders: hand-held and bench-mounted. The hand-held unit is very good for cutting and finishing in awkward areas, whereas the bench-mounted unit is designed for sharpening tools and shaping small items.

SAFETY NOTE

❏ Power tools can be lethal if not handled correctly. When using electric tools be extra careful. Never use them in damp or wet conditions. Always make sure that your work is well supported and that the sudden application of power will not make you lose your grip on it. Use safety goggles, face masks and ear protectors.

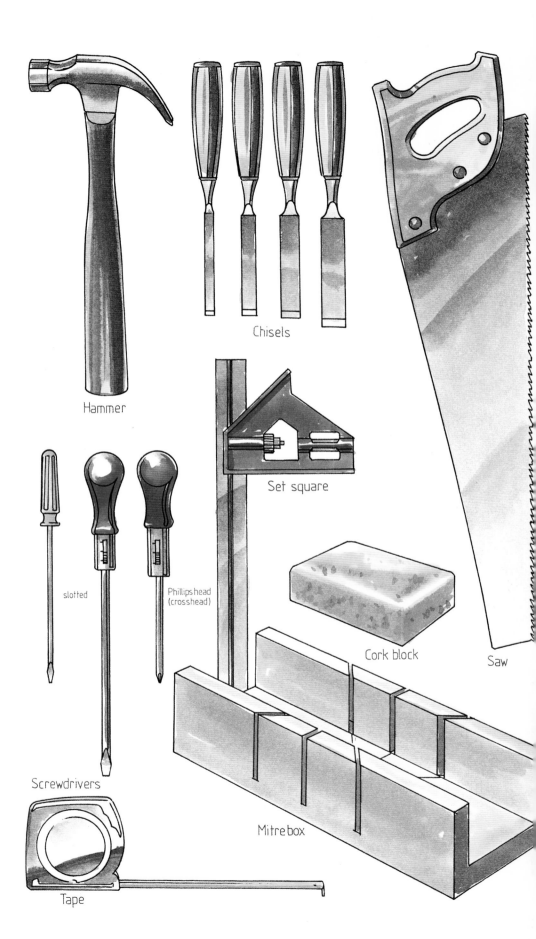

Hammer

Chisels

Set square

slotted

Phillips head (crosshead)

Cork block

Saw

Screwdrivers

Mitre box

Tape

Spirit level

File

Crowbar

G-clamp

Hacksaw

Knife

Pliers

Nail punch

Smoothing plane

Adjustable spanner

Chalk line

Circular saw

Electric drill

Jigsaw

Grinder

Sander

Electric screwdriver

TIPSTRIP

❑ Avoid cheap tools and always go for quality. Good, albeit expensive, tools should last forever and will be well worth the money.
❑ Most tools can take a beating but chisels, tape measures, spirit levels and planes must be carefully looked after. Chisels and plane blades can be restored with a whetstone and a steady hand.
❑ Phillips head (cross-head) screws that create their own holes when driven in with a power screwdriver (known in the trade as 'grabbers') can save a lot of time and effort when you have a large number of screws to fit.
❑ Never lend your tools to anyone. An annoying thing about tools is that they disappear, especially when there are strangers about.
❑ At all costs don't let tools stay wet if you get caught in the rain. A wipe over with an oily rag prevents rusting.
❑ When buying timber, never accept what is given to you without running your eye down the length of it to check for straightness and knots. Preferably choose your own, even if it takes longer.
❑ A tradesman's tip: treat any kind of burn with PVA adhesive the moment it occurs. Coat the wound liberally and allow to dry.

GENERAL TIPS FOR POWER TOOLS
❑ Buy the best you can afford.
❑ For very heavy jobs which might overtax your power tool, hire an industrial version.
❑ Keep blades/cutters/drills sharp.
❑ Discard chipped or damaged grinding discs and sanding discs/belts.
❑ Ensure blade guards and so on are in place before switching on.

You need more than money to create a kitchen that looks good and works well. Far more important is a sense of how you actually want your kitchen to work, plus a knowledge of basic planning principles.

THE KITCHEN PLAN

The layout of the room, rather than its size, has an enormous impact on its level of efficiency. It's worth taking your time over the planning stage to avoid what could prove to be costly and annoying mistakes.

There is no right or wrong design for a kitchen; if it suits the way you operate, then that's absolutely fine.

Before you call in a kitchen company, architect, designer or builder, it's worth thinking about how you want the kitchen to be used; probably not a subject you've given much thought to up until now.

Obviously its basic functions are in the cooking and serving of meals, and the cleaning up afterwards. However, the way all that works for you is a fairly complex matter, so first ask yourself the following questions:

❑ How many family members use the kitchen?
❑ Will more than one person be cooking in it at a time?
❑ What do you all like and dislike about your present kitchen?
❑ What is your idea of the ultimate kitchen?
❑ Do you eat in the kitchen, and if so, just for quick snacks or for sit-down meals?
❑ What eating facilities are needed: a table, a breakfast bar, or a fold-down table?
❑ Do you need a serving hatch through to the dining room?
❑ Is the kitchen the social centre of the house?
❑ What activities take place in the kitchen apart from food preparation and eating hot meals?
❑ Do the children do their homework or watch television in there?
❑ Do you want a casual sitting area for friends?
❑ Do you eat a lot of frozen food; in other words, do you need a separate freezer?
❑ Does it necessarily have to be in the kitchen?
❑ How much food and equipment do you keep in the kitchen?
❑ Will cutlery and crockery be kept in the kitchen or dining room?
❑ How much worktop do you need?
❑ Is your present kitchen big enough?
❑ Can you take in extra space from adjoining areas or rooms?
❑ Do you need to add an extension to your house to accommodate the new kitchen?
❑ Could you remove a wall or two between your current kitchen and an adjoining room?
❑ Could you re-site the kitchen in another room?
❑ What sort of power do you use for cooking?
❑ Do you need to change your power supplies?
❑ Are these changes vital, or would you be just as satisfied with another arrangement?
❑ Do you have enough power points for all your small appliances?
❑ How much money do you have to spend on your new kitchen?
❑ Will you have to borrow money?
❑ Are you thinking of moving within the next few years? If so, don't overspend. A sound investment would be to build a kitchen that costs no more than 10 per cent of the current resale value of your house.

These are the basics – from there you must think about materials you want to use in the kitchen, the look you are hoping to achieve, as well as more practical aspects such as lighting, waste disposal and ventilation. You'll find information on those things later in the book.

For the layout of your new kitchen, many people find it useful to draw up an accurate scale floor plan of the room on graph paper, and then make scale cut-outs of all appliances (with allowances for pipes, wires and ventilation). They can then be moved around on the plan, until you find the most suitable set-up for your needs. If you find it hard to visualise on paper, you can do the same thing in the actual kitchen, using masking tape to show where cupboards and appliances will go.

TIPSTRIP

In an eat-in kitchen, install a dimmer switch for the light over the dining table, so that lighting can be atmospheric for formal meals, and brightened for schoolwork. Similarly, a rise-and-fall pendant light over the table can be raised and lowered to create different effects.

A modern country look – this kitchen features attractive and practical storage areas

The eat-in kitchen

The most informal arrangement, the eat-in kitchen can fit into almost any shaped room as long as it's not too small.

A great benefit of this layout is that the cook need never feel left out from what's going on at the table. On the down side of things it is impossible to close the door on kitchen mess.

The most usual configuration is to have a single-line or L-shaped kitchen, with the table in the middle of the room. When not in use, it can double as extra workspace, acting as an island in the room. You must be sure to leave at least one metre around the perimeter of the table to accommodate chairs. If space is a problem, consider having benches instead of chairs; they are not as flexible, but take up less room.

Another possibility, in a narrower room, is to have a single-line arrangement with the table against the opposite wall. Make sure, if there are overhead cupboards or shelves on this wall, that they are not directly above the chairs.

With both these types of eat-in kitchen, try to find a dining table that complements the overall design of the room. For instance, in a country-style kitchen, you could choose an old scrubbed pine table; in a modern setting a simple ash or marble-topped table may be more appropriate. In many kitchens, there's not the space for a proper table; the dining part of the room, then, may be a peninsula unit, or small return at the end of a sweep of worktop.

You may need to look for fold-up chairs, which can be stored away neatly when not in use, or stools, which can tuck away under the bar. Another possibility is to have a breakfast bar running along the length of the room in a narrow single-line kitchen. If space is at a premium, the bar can be hinged so that it folds down against the wall when it is not being used.

In a really tiny kitchen, the top drawer in a bank of drawers can conceal a pull-out table, which can also be used as extra worktop space when necessary.

A spacious L-shaped eat-in kitchen

Poggenpohl – Kitchen Architecture

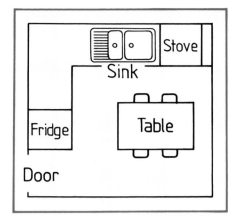
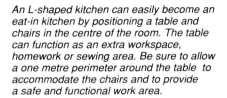

An L-shaped kitchen can easily become an eat-in kitchen by positioning a table and chairs in the centre of the room. The table can function as an extra workspace, homework or sewing area. Be sure to allow a one metre perimeter around the table to accommodate the chairs and to provide a safe and functional work area.

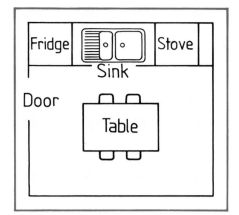

Single-line kitchens maximise space and allow room for a dining area. If the bench area of the kitchen is inadequate the table can be used as an extra work surface. As with all eat-in kitchens, allow for the traffic flow by positioning the table and chairs so that at least one person can be working in the kitchen while others are seated.

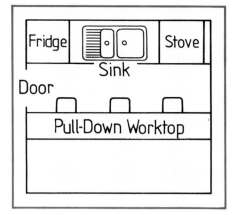

When space is a problem a pull-down hinged surface can be incorporated into a single-line kitchen to create an eating area or extra worktop. Stools or folding chairs are best as they can be removed when the worktop is folded away, to increase the floor space. This handy work surface, when in use, creates a flexible galley-style kitchen.

THE WORK TRIANGLE

It's been around for years, and although cliched, the so-called work triangle is a good starting point in the planning of your kitchen. In essence, it's a way of organising elements so that the room can be used in the most efficient way.

Admittedly, not everyone demands the same thing from a kitchen, and with technological advances such as the microwave oven and dishwasher, priorities have changed over the years and the kitchen in general is used in a different way. However, the basic principles still apply.

The three major items in the kitchen are cooker, sink and refrigerator. These should be placed in a triangle, with the sink as the pivot point. Ideally, the triangle should be equilateral with sides of no less than 1.2 m, otherwise you will feel too cramped. Likewise, they should be no more

than a couple of metres apart to avoid unnecessary walking.

If you decide on a cooktop (hob) and wall oven, and perhaps a microwave, it's not always possible to group them together in the work triangle. In that case, it's probably a good idea to have the cooktop (hob) in the triangle, with the wall oven built into a bank of cupboards. The microwave oven, which doesn't take up much room, can be placed on the worktop, mounted on a swivelling wall bracket, or built into a bank of cupboards. Remember to have it at a low enough level so that all the family can use it.

Another consideration is the dishwasher – even if you don't plan to install one straight away it's a good idea to make provision for one. That way, later plumbing and installation costs can be minimised. Ideally, it should be placed near the sink, within easy reach of cupboards in which crockery and glassware are stored.

For safety, the triangle

should not be interrupted by a doorway; someone racing in unexpectedly could easily cause an accident.

Between each of the three appliances there should be sufficient work surface for

preparing and cleaning up after meals. A set down space of at least half a metre should be allocated beside the refrigerator and stove for safety as well as convenience.

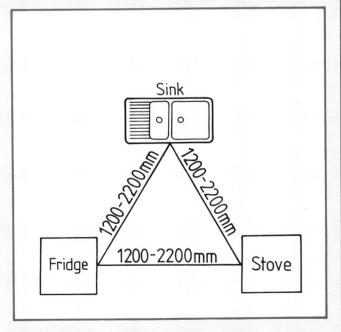

The L-shaped kitchen

This configuration is suitable for virtually all types of rooms, except for particularly narrow ones, or those with lots of doors.

It's often used to create a kitchen in the corner of an open-plan living room, or in a large combined kitchen/dining room.

In almost every case, the L-shaped kitchen can include an eating area, even if it's only in the form of a breakfast bar; generally, though, there's room here for a table. Of course, it's a very sociable set-up, ideal for relaxed entertaining and family meals, enabling the cook to join in conversation without feeling excluded. It's also an adaptable arrangement, which should easily be able to accommodate two cooks at a time, and one in which through traffic is generally not a problem.

There are several possible configurations for the L-shaped kitchen. It can run along two adjacent walls, meeting in the corner – this is particularly suitable in the case of a large eat-in kitchen. Another possibility is that all appliances run along one arm of the 'L', with the other arm forming a peninsula unit or divider between the kitchen and the living or dining area.

The temptation, if the room is very large, is to make the sides of the 'L' extra long, stretching out the work triangle. The message is to keep the work triangle fairly compact, but separated by reasonable stretches of worktop to ensure that the main working area doesn't get too congested. In order to gain a convenient sweep of unbroken workspace, the refrigerator and tall cupboards can be placed at either end of the two arms of the 'L', or at one end of the long arm. As in all other types of kitchen, the refrigerator should be placed in the most convenient position

The L-shape is a very sociable set-up.

for family members to use without getting in the cook's way.

Planning of the kitchen should include provision for a convenient setdown area near the stove, pantry or refrigerator, so that food can be moved safely and easily from one area to another.

Lighting is often a problem in the L-shaped kitchen, as a large proportion of worktop is likely to be away from the window. For this reason, leave the window uncluttered to maximise light during the day, and carefully plan overall and spot lighting so the kitchen is well lit at night.

WORKING WITH THE PROFESSIONALS

The first thing to do is to ask around amongst friends for recommendations of architects, kitchen specialists, interior designers and builders. Also, look in design magazines to find the names of people or companies whose work you admire. Make sure whoever you choose is qualified to do the job.

Obtain quotes from at least three builders to compare prices. Beware of the difference between a firm quote – a fixed price – and an estimate, which is just an educated guess at the final cost.

The cheapest quote is not necessarily the one you should choose; ask to see an example of the builder's work, and try to talk to previous clients.

Be specific when you're asking for quotes; put in as many details as possible. For instance, if you want a particular laminate, say so; otherwise the builder will almost certainly price the job on the cheapest available material. Even so, when the work is finished, you can expect a price variation of anything up to 15 per cent on your original quote.

The work done by builders, kitchen companies, interior designers and architects varies enormously. Clarify exactly what can be expected of them – will they be supervising the job, for example, or merely drawing up plans.

Ask for a written work schedule from the builder, and don't be satisfied with 'about 10 days'. Insist on details such as 'removing existing kitchen – one man, one day; electrical work – one man, half a day'. Find out how the builder wants to be paid; the usual way is at the completion of each stage. This is where the work schedule comes in handy. Some small businesses, however, do not have the cash flow to buy materials without being paid up front.

Find out about professional fees. Are they a flat fee, or a percentage of the cost of the job? Make sure you find this out before the work starts, so that you don't have any nasty surprises later on.

Find out how many men will be permanently on site, and what they expect working hours to be.

Establish the order of work; find out, for instance, whether the plumber can come early if the electrician fails to turn up on time.

Ask the builder to give you a completion date, and have a penalty clause written into the contract making the builder liable for any unacceptable delays. He cannot be held responsible for acts of God, for unforeseen situations such as a major damp problem, or for any change of mind you may have.

Clarify the day-to-day arrangements the builder has; where he will store his material (you don't want him blocking access to your garage); what access there is to the site – if it's through the house, make sure the floors are protected; whether he will use your bathroom and telephone, or make his own arrangements. Always add a final stage to the building schedule, relating to making good, detail work and clearing up. This will give the builder the incentive not to abandon you at an awkward moment. It could include such things as rehanging doors which do not open properly or repairing faulty switches.

Right: The breakfast bar can double as a room divider Far right: The L-shape is particularly suitable as an eat-in kitchen

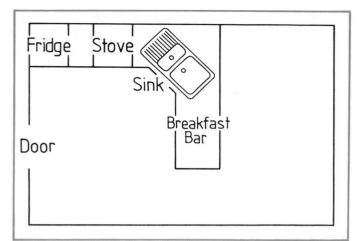

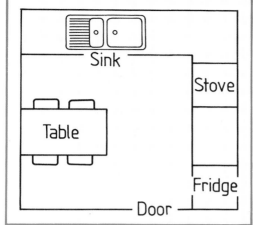

Several possible configurations exist for the L-shaped kitchen. It can run along two adjacent walls, meeting in the corner – this is particularly suitable in the case of a large eat-in kitchen. Another possibility is that all appliances run along one arm of the 'L', with the other arm forming a peninsula unit or divider between the kitchen, living or dining area.

Right: The compact work area of this L-shaped kitchen includes modern appliances and a breakfast bar

IKEA

The U-shaped kitchen

With cabinets and appliances running in an unbroken line around three counters, the U-shape is generally considered to be the most workable kitchen design.

To create an efficient work triangle in a U-shaped kitchen, awkwardly positioned doorways are more of a problem than the actual size of the room. In the true U-shape, the line of work surfaces is uninterrupted by doors, so that the cook is undisturbed by family members continually tramping through the work area.

A small kitchen can happily accommodate a U-shape, although it is important that the floor space between the two arms be at least 1.5 m, and preferably 1.8 m if there is

likely to be more than one person working in there at any one time.

A large U-shape can, admittedly, offer a large expanse of worktop, but, unless you're careful, it can also create an elongated work triangle. It's best to confine the triangle to the base of the 'U', unless you want the walking you do in the kitchen to contribute significantly to your overall exercise program!

Apart from considering the work triangle, it's also important to consider plumbing requirements –

keeping changes to original plumbing to a minimum. You will also have to think about access to gas and electricity, and the need to allow enough room for all doors to open comfortably.

The most common configuration is to have the sink at the base of the 'U', with cooker and refrigerator facing each other on the arms. It's advisable to place the refrigerator as near as possible to the kitchen doorway, so that family members can get to it without disturbing the cook. If you plan to have a dishwasher, it could either be placed near the sink, or on the same arm as the refrigerator.

With the continuous sweep of worktop found in the U-shaped kitchen, it's often possible to fit in a tall larder and broom cupboard. The usual rule applies here – put them at

each end of the 'U' to avoid breaking up the work surface. Alternatively, if there's a fourth wall in the kitchen, the taller items (including, if you like, a wall oven or refrigerator as well as storage cupboards) can be placed here, linked, perhaps by an appliance centre. Often, that fourth wall is separated from the 'U' by a well-used traffic way. If that's the case, for safety reasons, the walkway should be at least 1.1 m wide, and the wall oven should have an off-loading counter beside it.

In a U-shaped kitchen it is often possible to fit in a spot for eating, even if it's only a bar along one leg of the 'U'. If this is separated by a tall unit from the working area, it could be at a lower level to suit children.

The U-shaped kitchen is not necessarily self-contained; often there is no fourth wall, and instead, the kitchen interconnects with another room. Another common situation is that units and appliances run along two walls, and the third arm makes up a room divider. The area above the divider can be left completely open; the divider then becomes a serving surface, or perhaps even a breakfast bar.

Left: The true U-shaped kitchen can be varied to accommodate doorways and appliances while still offering a large expanse of workspace
Below: Four different U-shaped configurations

Alternatively, open shelving or a high divider can partly screen the work zone from the living or dining area. This way, the cook can still see what's going on, but any mess can be hidden.

It's a good idea if the units which make up the divider have doors opening into both areas; for instance, if there's a dining table on one side, store all crockery on that side, while cooking utensils would be better kept in the part which opens to the kitchen.

As in many types of kitchen, corners are a problem in the U-shape. Most manufacturers include corner units in

their ranges; carousels for wall or base units, and units with bifold doors. Especially in a small kitchen, it's important to squeeze in as much storage as possible; efficient use of tricky corners can give valuable extra space. If a corner unit backs onto a dining area, doors that open on the dining side will allow full access to it.

It's also important to make sure that doors don't open into each other, and that appliances such as refrigerators are placed at least 30 cm in from the corners so that doors can be opened completely, without banging into the walls.

A large U-shape can offer a large expanse of worktop, but, if you're not careful, it can also create an elongated work triangle. It's best to confine the triangle to the base of the 'U', unless you want all the walking you do in the kitchen to contribute to your overall exercise program.

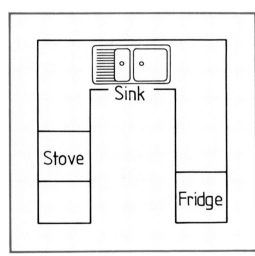

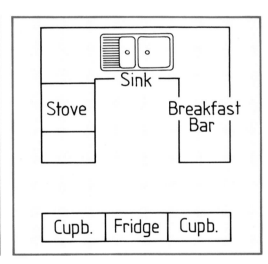

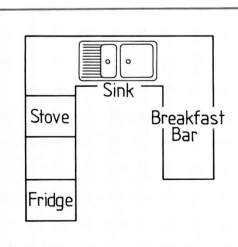

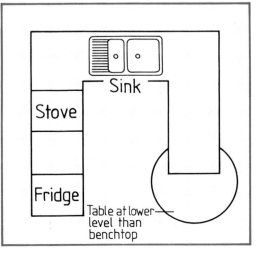

The single-line kitchen

If space is a problem, the single-line layout may be the most practical and efficient arrangement.

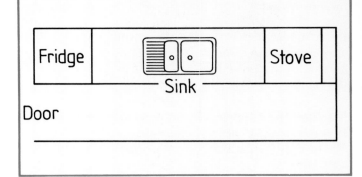

It's a challenge to the designer, but if planned carefully, the single-line kitchen can look neat, and work as well as a beautifully designed machine. In a multi-purpose room, it has the advantage of being able to be contained in one area, leaving most of the floor space free for dining and/or relaxing.

The main thing with a single-line kitchen, especially in a small area, is to allow as much worktop space as possible. To do this, you will need to be flexible in your choice of appliances and in your approach to storage. A built-under refrigerator and a cooktop (hob) with a pull-down cover give extra work space. There are dozens of styles of sinks available with chopping boards and drainer baskets; these are particularly handy when space is at a premium.

The most usual configuration in the single-line kitchen is for the sink to be in the middle of the worktop area with refrigerator and cooker on either side. For convenience, the refrigerator door, and the oven door (if it's a side-opening one), should open away from the sink. Most refrigerators offer the option of doors that open from either the left- or right-hand-side. If you have a dishwasher, place it next to the sink for easy access and to minimise plumbing costs. With a dishwasher, you may be able to manage with a sink without draining board.

Use every inch of wall space for storage; hang cupboards where possible, making sure that they are at least 60 cm above the work surface. To create a finished look, and to maximise storage, take all wall cupboards up to the ceiling. If the kitchen is in a corridor-type room, use the opposite wall for narrow shelving, fitted from floor to ceiling. Incorporate a fold-down shelf or table which can be used at breakfast time, for light snacks, or for handy extra workspace.

Above: Single-line kitchens require imaginative use of storage space
Below: A single-line kitchen is the best solution when space is at a premium

The galley kitchen

The galley kitchen, generally a narrow room with cabinets on the two long walls, is one of the most difficult types of kitchen to make work satisfactorily.

The most awkward arrangement is when the room is essentially a passageway between the back door and the main living areas. Much less troublesome is the corridor with one completely enclosed end wall, in which the only traffic is that coming into, and not through, the room.

In either case, there should be at least 1.2 m between the facing units, to allow two people to work together comfortably in the room and also, when it is a thoroughfare to the back door, to enable the family to walk through without getting too much in the cook's way. Any narrower than 1.2 m means that bending down to get something from a base unit would become a contortionist's feat, and it would also be impossible to simultane-

ously open doors on opposite sides of the room. If you have the space, a walkway of between 1.5 and 1.8 m is ideal. Much more than that and the working spaces are too far apart.

The most usual, and usable, arrangement for the galley kitchen is for the sink and cooker to be on one side with the refrigerator and storage on the opposite wall.

Alternatively, the refrigerator and sink can be on one side, with cooker on the other. If possible, place the refrigerator at the end of the kitchen most accessible to other rooms, so that everyone can use it without disturbing the cook. Work areas and appliances should be grouped together in such a way that you are not continually crossing the room. For

instance, the dishwasher should, if possible, be near the sink and crockery storage cupboards.

One great advantage of the galley kitchen is the potential for expanses of workspace. As is the rule with all styles of kitchen, locate tall items such as the refrigerator and broom cupboard at the ends of the walls to allow for uninterrupted sweeps of worktop.

The most usual, and usable, arrangement for the galley kitchen is for the sink and stove to be on one side with the refrigerator and storage on the opposite wall.

Elizabeth Whiting and Associates

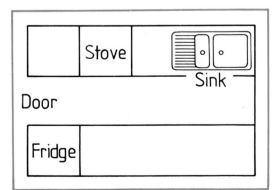

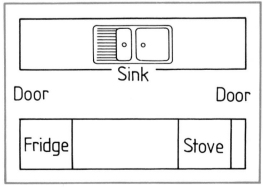

Above: A galley kitchen is like a narrow corridor, and utilises wall space with cupboards extending to the ceiling
Left: The galley kitchen's main advantage is the expanse of workspace it offers

Project 1

Fold-down table

A small kitchen may not have enough room for a permanent table at which a couple of people can eat breakfast or quick kitchen meals, but it may have a wall to which a fold-down table could be attached.

MATERIALS	
60 x 60 mm DAR (PAR) softwood tabletop as discussed piano hinge 2 regular hinges of the best quality caselock, as used for musical instrument cases spring latch masonry bolts or screws and plugs locking stay paint or lacquer	

TOOLS	TIME
spanner screwdrivers handsaw and/or power saw drill spadebit and masonry bit	1-2 days

Such a table can also provide extra workspace when needed as well as a place for family and friends to sit and keep the cook company while meals are being prepared. Folding chairs, some kind of cosy lighting arrangement and a spot for a small television on a facing wall could make previously dead space the most popular spot in the house.

Before making any decisions about the size of the table, decide on your chairs and place them in situ, working out whether you actually have enough space and what restrictions the table will place on movement in the kitchen. Bear in mind that a comfortable minimum width must allow two people to sit opposite each other without banging knees.

The distance the table protrudes from the wall depends on its height as it cannot be so long that it won't fold down flush against the wall. About 72 cm plus the mounting block is about right (see fig. 1) but test it with the chairs you intend to use.

The tabletop could be made from a variety of materials, depending on availability and your tools. Possibilities include:
❑ 25-30 mm thick fibreboard (MDF) which you could buy cut to size at a timber yard, or cut it yourself using a circular saw and a clamped straightedge as a guide. Clamp the sheet to a bench or table to stop it shifting when you make your cut. Draw the line along which the cut is to be made then establish where your straightedge needs to be clamped. It will be parallel to the cut line at a distance which is determined by the distance from the blade of your circular saw to the edge of its baseplate, which will be pushed along the straightedge during the cut. Experiment on some scrap sheet to get that distance exactly right. (See fig. 4).

The surface finish could be either high- or low-gloss enamel paint or a laminate, although a laminate could be as easily applied to regular coarse grain particle (chip) board (see box).

❑ Glued and clamped pine lengths (90 or 120 x 40 mm). Sash cramps are needed for this and the amount of surface sanding required depends very much on the straightness of the timber. Sometimes cabinet makers can be persuaded, for a nominal fee, to surface-sand such items in their big belt sanders. The assembly should be glued together first, with PVA adhesive, and cut to size afterwards, using the same technique as for fibreboard. The surface may be finished with either paint or lacquer. Be sure to clean excess adhesive off the surface before it dries as it is very difficult to remove when dry.

As we are proposing only a fairly small table here, one leg should be sufficient, although two may be fitted if desired. One leg has the advantage of allowing easier access for people and chairs.

STEP BY STEP

1 Cut a length of 60 x 60 mm timber to the desired width of the table. This is the block from which the table will be hinged and which will be fastened to the wall. If it is a stud wall use at least two 80 mm coach screws, counterbored 20 mm or so with a spadebit in a drill, secured into separate stud beams. If it is a brick wall use masonry bolts of the same length or greater, also counterbored 20 mm. When using masonry bolts be sure to drill to the exact depth the bolts will be inserted and hammer them in until solid contact is made with the bottom of the hole, or the bolts will not grab properly.

You can use various types of hinge but a piano hinge which runs the length of the block is recommended (see fig. 2). Other types of hinge require rebates to be made in the mounting block.

2 The leg will be too long to fold between the tabletop and the wall so it is cut and hinged. Where you make the cut is up to you but halfway is recommended. Use 60 x 60 mm timber for the leg and chamfer each corner to about 5 mm. When the leg is supporting the table it is fixed into one rigid length with the aid of a caselock on the side opposite to that with the hinge (see fig. 3). A caselock is often used on musical instrument cases and camera cases, available at well-stocked ironmongers. For appearance the caselock and

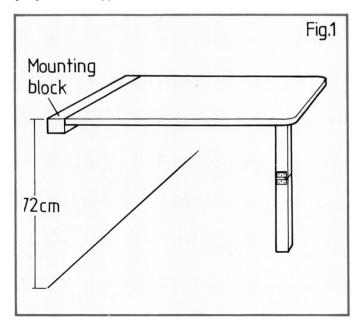

Fig.1

Mounting block

72cm

the hinge should preferably be made of the same metal. Rebate for both hinges. Where the top hinge connects with the underside of the tabletop a rebate is not strictly necessary although it would improve the firmness of the joint.

3 All that is now required is to clip the folded leg to the underside of the table for when it is folded down against the wall and not in use. Some kind of ball and spring cupboard door latch can be used although your DIY shop will have a variety to choose from. A locking stay is also required to stop the leg from folding under when the table is in use (see fig. 3).

4 Painting should be done very carefully in a dust-free environment with a good quality gloss paint. For toughness, at least three coats with a light sand between each one is required. For extra toughness you can even finish with a couple of coats of lacquer. Remember that time spent sanding all components will be well rewarded with a superior finish.

Right: Circular saw with blade guard omitted to show where to place straightedge to make a cut

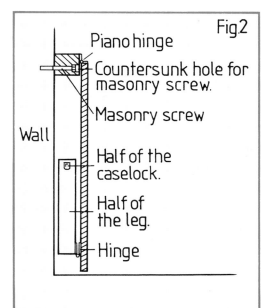

Fig.2

- Piano hinge
- Countersunk hole for masonry screw.
- Masonry screw
- Half of the caselock.
- Half of the leg.
- Hinge

Wall

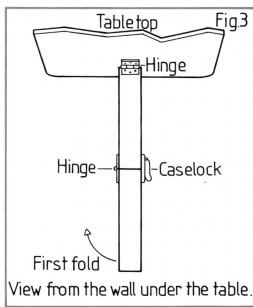

Fig.3

Table top

- Hinge
- Hinge
- Caselock
- First fold

View from the wall under the table.

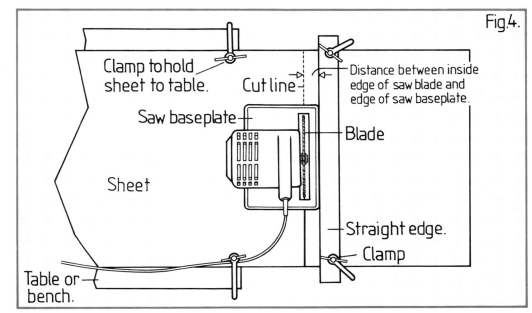

Fig.4.

- Clamp to hold sheet to table.
- Cut line
- Distance between inside edge of saw blade and edge of saw baseplate.
- Saw baseplate
- Blade
- Sheet
- Straight edge.
- Clamp
- Table or bench.

APPLYING LAMINATE TO PARTICLE (CHIP) BOARD

Draw the pieces you want on the decorative side of your laminate sheet, allowing sufficient extra on the surface piece for the strips that will be glued to the edges.

Use a square and double check your measurements. If unsure of how much extra to allow for the thickness of the laminate on the edges, first cut off a couple of pieces to experiment. The contact adhesive, if applied correctly, will add about 0.5 mm.

Score along your lines with a laminate cutter, a simple and cheap device with a tungsten carbide tip. Once you have achieved a good clean break through the laminate's decorative surface, break the sheet along a straightedge, applying downward pressure over the whole length of the cut. It should snap in two along the score line, after which the backing, which may be jagged on the edge, can be sanded smooth. You may even want to try

sanding it back at an angle with a sanding block for a mitred join.

Cover both surfaces to be joined with a thin and even coat of thixotropic contact adhesive, making sure to avoid lumps, and wait until the adhesive dries to a tacky, almost dry feeling. Line up the laminate carefully and press it onto the particle (chip) board a bit at a time, making full use of the laminate's flexibility, and smoothing it firmly with a cloth.

A drawing pin pushed into the edge will assist in positioning the top surface laminate. Once the two glued surfaces come into contact you are fully committed to your positioning because contact adhesive works like its name: full adhesion is achieved with contact.

Add your edge pieces and clean excess adhesive off the laminate with the manufacturer's recommended solvent as soon as possible.

Gone are the days when the kitchen was a purely utilitarian room. Today we put as much thought into the look of our kitchens as we do to any other part of the house.

KITCHEN STYLES

Once you've finalised the floor plan of your new kitchen, you can concentrate on the style. Are you after a comfortable and cosy look, or something more streamlined? Here we look at the elements found in various types of kitchen – combine them to suit your own style.

Country

As soon as you walk into the country kitchen, it's as if there's a huge welcome mat at the door. You see it in the lovely comfortable clutter, the warm timber, the informality and the deliberately mismatched old tiles in the splashback. Bowls of fruit and vegetables on display – perhaps just one type, such as lemons or pears – indicate a love of nature. Herbs and spices are decanted into pretty jars; farmhouse loaves sit on the breadboard; wire baskets full of eggs add to the mood.

The first impression may be that while it's appealing to look at, it doesn't work very well. That need not be the case at all; as long as the country kitchen is designed carefully, there is no reason why it need not be every bit as efficient as any other type of kitchen.

One of the most vital aspects of the country kitchen is storage. While in many other styles of kitchen, the idea is to hide everything away, it's just the opposite for the country look. A dresser can be used to show off collections of china or glassware; a similar effect can also be achieved with open shelving. A large plate rack built in above the sink gives a definite country feel, but also serves a very useful purpose, doubling as draining rack and storage space. A rack suspended by chains from a crossbeam or joist provides valuable extra storage space. Buy one ready-made, or make your own from lengths of piping or broom handles, and use butchers' hooks or cup hooks to hang anything, from copper pans to dried herbs.

What country kitchen would be complete without a large walk-in pantry, lined with shelves? It's a nostalgic, as well as an entirely practical, option.

Of course, timber is the predominant material in the country kitchen. Tongue-and-groove cupboard doors finished with matt lacquer or, if you're a perfectionist, waxed, give an authentic feel. A butcher's block can be used for a worktop, and it looks especially good to mix light and dark timbers, to give the impression that the kitchen has evolved rather than been built in one go.

You can even use timber on the floor, but terracotta, flagstone, slate or earthy-coloured tiles are just as appropriate and are easier to maintain.

As in any other kitchen, you should also be concerned about getting in as much natural light as possible. A stable door would be the obvious choice here, especially if it leads onto a lovely outside eating area. If that's not suitable, consider installing a skylight, french windows or a glass door, large windows or a bank of smaller ones.

A mesh-front cupboard with small drawers and a plate and mug rack

Cabinetcraft Kitchens

Leadlight and shelves with wooden rails add character to a country kitchen

Cabinetcraft Kitchens

As long as the country kitchen is designed carefully, there is no reason why it need not be as efficient as any other type of kitchen.

Rangewood Kitchens

Cabinetcraft Kitchens

Above: Shelves and a drawer are an attractive feature for a kitchen corner
Below: A country kitchen featuring wood cupboards, leadlight and patterned wall tiles

Above: A dresser is a way to include extra storage and display areas

Cabinetcraft Kitchens

Ultra-modern

Is it a space station, is it a laboratory – no, it's a kitchen, an ultra-modern one. Here you'll find the best of everything, the very latest technology. No room here for comfortable clutter – everything's hidden from view, or displayed purely for its functional qualities. Small appliances sit in purpose-built cabinets, always close at hand – the message here is efficiency, speed and streamlining.

Materials for the ultra-modern kitchen are chosen for their practical attributes; worktops of stainless steel are hygienic and easy to look after, as too are the stainless steel splashbacks. For a particularly streamlined effect the whole worktop, including sink and draining board, are moulded out of one piece of stainless steel. Alternatively, use granite for a sleek worktop. Colour can come into its own in the ultra-modern kitchen. If you've got the courage, the sky's the limit – the more vibrant, the better. Be bold, this room can take it.

Take your ideas for storage from the commercial world – use metal shelving, industrial systems, wire grids. Steal inspiration from the chemistry laboratory to give your ultra-modern kitchen the serious look – deep sinks, winged taps, glass beakers and glass-stoppered storage jars. Cupboards should look sleek and unadorned. Choose one of the new iridescent laminates, or MDF with a durable polyurethane finish.

For flooring, tough rubber gives a suitably industrial effect. For over-the-top modern, use it on walls too. For something a little more restrained, and as a foil to the super-efficient laboratory look, choose timber boards, parquet, or plain coloured ceramic tiles.

The ultra-modern look is not for the fainthearted; it's the home of the brave.

Take your ideas for storage from the commercial world – metal shelving, industrial systems, wire grids. Steal inspiration from the chemistry laboratory to give your ultra-modern kitchen the serious look – deep sinks, winged taps, glass beakers and glass stoppered jars.

An ultra-modern kitchen that combines stainless steel with dark surfaces to give a dramatic and unusual effect

Kitchen Architecture

Kitchen Architecture

Kitchen Architecture

Above: A midway storage shelf
Right: A large butcher's block, with a rack for hanging kitchen implements and shelves above and below

Below: An ultra-modern kitchen is devoid of clutter and features streamlined walls, appliances in purpose-built cabinets, hygienic surfaces and the very latest in kitchen technology

Poggenpohl – Kitchen Architecture

Family

By definition, the family kitchen is expansive; the hub of the house where everyone can get together to eat, to talk, to cook, or just to relax. For the cook who hates to feel isolated, this is the answer. It's a room which should take the whole family into consideration; tough enough to deal with the kids, comfortable enough for everyone.

Planning is vital; clearly defined areas and traffic patterns have to be established to avoid chaos. The cook has to be able to work happily in a carefully-designed food preparation area without fear of children underfoot as they make a beeline for the refrigerator or sink.

Try to incorporate an area for the children to do their homework (perhaps the dining table can double as a desk); a comfortable seating spot for friends and family to relax; a couple of stools near a worktop so that guests can have a drink, and maybe even lend a hand while you're preparing a meal.

If you've got the space, an area in the family kitchen can be set aside for watching television, for bookshelves, for hobbies. A lovely touch, which would add atmosphere to the room, would be to build in a fireplace.

Because this is the most well-used room in the house, orientate it, if you're in at the planning stages, towards the best view, the sunniest outlook. If you can install french windows opening to a balcony, garden or patio, so much the better.

Choose the most hardwearing surfaces you can possibly find – this is certainly not the place for fragile materials. It's a room that will work hard for you, and should answer your every demand.

Planning is vital; establish clearly defined areas and traffic patterns to avoid chaos. The cook has to be able to work happily in a carefully designed food preparation area without fear of children underfoot as they make a beeline for the refrigerator or sink.

The family kitchen – a place where everyone can gather, that features expansive work areas and plenty of room for a busy traffic flow

Professional

The professional kitchen can take on many guises – at first glance it can look like a country kitchen or an ultra-modern kitchen, even a family kitchen, or anything in between. It's only at closer inspection that you realise there are things here which set it apart – you can see that whoever's in control here really is in control. This is the working environment for someone who's not beaten by soufflés, and for whom cooking is far more than just slinging a few chops under the grill at the last minute.

The professional kitchen is an individual room – the design of it depends entirely on the person using it. It'll be the sort of kitchen in which everything has a place, but apart from that, it can vary enormously. The sink will probably need to be larger than average to accommodate large commercial cooking equipment. Many professional (and enthusiastic amateur) cooks find an extra sink indispensable. Perhaps this can be set in a central island away from the main working area; or it could be handy to the vegetable preparation area.

A bank of ovens is also a popular choice – perhaps one regular, the other fan forced; or one gas, the other electric. An alternative would be to have a capacious professional range. A microwave oven will almost certainly find its way into this kitchen too.

If the cook is catering for large numbers of people, extra storage will be needed to house larger-than-average equipment – baking trays, casserole dishes and so on. The normal household refrigerator is far from adequate for the professional cook – two refrigerators standing side by side may be more suitable, or even a commercial glass-fronted refrigerator, the type more commonly found in take-away and grocery stores.

Everything has to work here – you'll need the best ventilation system possible to clear cooking smells; all equipment will be top quality; and the design of the kitchen has to be functional above all, to keep extra work to a minimum. Materials will be tough and easy to look after – the practical side of things is top of the list.

TIPSTRIP

A midway wall storage unit is perfect for storing sharp kitchen implements such as food processor blades. Not only does it keep them in easy reach (absolutely necessary for the serious cook), but it is also a much safer way of storing them than in a drawer.

Midway units, attached to the wall between the worktop and the wall cupboards, can also be used for holding jars of fresh herbs, condiments, seasonings, or any other often-used ingredients.

Kitchen Architecture

The professional kitchen is an individual room – the design of it depends entirely on the person using it. It will be the sort of kitchen in which everything has a place, but apart from that, it can vary enormously.

Right: A midway storage rack for kitchen implements
Below: A professional kitchen varied to include an eating area. It still incorporates modern storage systems and appliances which are hidden from view
Below left: Stainless steel and wood are combined to give a hygienic work area. Like most professional kitchens an extra sink is included to accommodate the amount of cooking equipment

Kitchen Architecture

Kitchen Architecture

Project 2

Installing a kit kitchen

TTT

So you have decided to do it yourself. You have designed it around your lifestyle, your budget and the range that is available. It has finally arrived in cartons and your new kitchen is only hours (or days) away.

First take the time to go through the cartons to check that what you've got is what you ordered. Don't try to adapt something to fit, because manufacturers will not exchange goods once they have been modified or altered from the original specification.

Make sure the kitchen is ready: have the walls been repaired? Do you need to change your plumbing? Should you move your power points or light switches or add more? Has the plumbing and electrical work been organised for the dishwasher, new wall oven or cooktop (hob)?

Finally, consider the height of the person who will be working in the kitchen when deciding on how high the worktops and wall cupboards should be.

STEP BY STEP
Floor units
1 Assemble all the cabinet carcasses following the manufacturer's instructions to the letter. Do not attach cupboard doors until the kitchen has been completely fitted.

2 Check the level of the floor to determine whether the base requires packing or planing.

To do this, run a pencil or chalk line around the wall at the height the cabinets will finish – usually 870-900 mm but it may be higher or lower. Alternatively, use a spirit level (see fig. 1). Also check whether the cabinets are on adjustable legs.

3 Check walls for plumb and straightness using a straightedge and/or a spirit level (see fig. 2), or a length of string and a weight.

4 Check walls for square, using 3:4:5 method (i.e. from the corner, measure 3 units – metres, yards or an arbitrary unit of measurement – along one wall and 4 units along the other. If the corner is a right angle the distance between the two marked points, the hypotenuse, will be 5 units.) (see fig. 3).

5 Begin with a corner cabinet. Set the cabinet in the corner, pack it with wedges until it is level but do not raise the cabinet above the line. Now take a pencil and scribe a line around your cabinet at the wall and floor. Alternatively, pack the gaps so that when fixed into position the cabinet still sits square and level (see fig. 4).

6 Plane the edges so that they run parallel with the scribed line. Use a no. 4.5 smoothing

plane or electric planer, taking care not to break out edges and corners. When fitted, fix back to the wall with the correct fasteners (masonry plugs and screws, or just screws) at two points around the top of the cabinet.

7 Repeat the last process for the next cabinet, ensuring that it joins neatly to the corner unit and that the front edges and top line up flush.

Wall oven and pantry units
End panels are supplied for most wall oven and pantry units separately, and these need to be attached to the assembled pantry/wall oven before the cabinets are installed. Installation procedure for wall oven/ pantry units is the same as for floor units.

Worktops
Most prefabricated worktops have joints at the major corners. The usual method of holding the joints together is with toggles (see fig. 5). The toggles fit into recesses precut into the underside of the worktop. Tightening the toggles can present some difficulty for fixing. But to begin, we will start by fitting a length of worktop.

Check the floor level with a spirit level

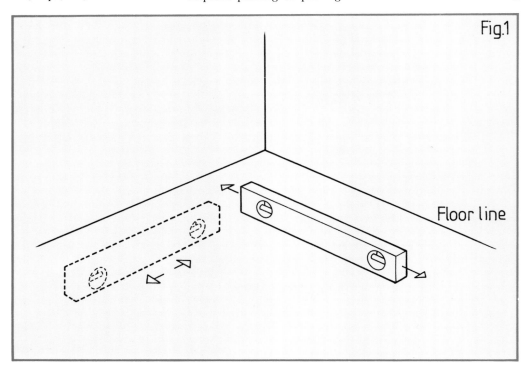

Fig.1

Floor line

MATERIALS
kit kitchen
silicone sealant

TOOLS
spirit level
screwdriver or power driver
chalk line
square
hammer and mallet
power saw
plane (manual or electric)
clamps
drill and bits

TIME
2-3 days

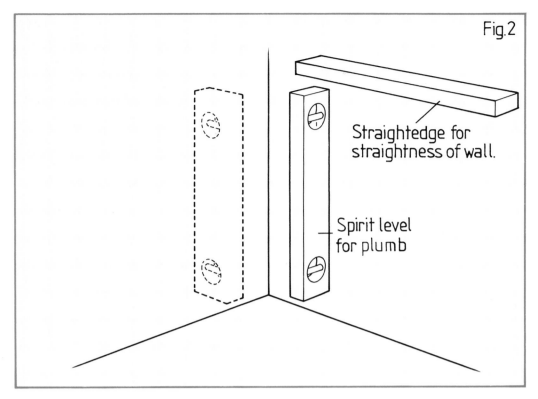

Fig.2

Straightedge for straightness of wall.

Spirit level for plumb

1 Mark the worktop length carefully. Use an electric planer or smoothing plane if only a small amount needs to be trimmed. If a a large section has to be removed, score first with a laminate knife to just below the coloured outer surface of the laminate, then trim with a jigsaw, power saw or handsaw, cutting on the waste side of the line (see fig. 6).

2 Scribe the back edge and plane to fit. Do not touch any pre-machined joints. With the worktop fitted, wedge it into place temporarily. Fit the next piece as above but, as before, do not attempt to alter any premachined joints.

3 After fitting all pieces, raise worktops about 150 mm above the tops of the cabinets. Make sure you support them on bearers of some kind.

4 Coat each joint with silicone sealant before bringing joints together. This prevents water

penetration and stops the laminate from lifting.

5 After tightening all toggle joints, carefully remove all bearers and fix the worktop into place with screws (not too long). Run a line of silicone sealant around the wall/ worktop joints.

Wall units
Fitting wall units is the same as for floor units except that you don't need to scribe anything to the floor. You should run a level line around your walls in the same way as you have done for your base units. Before you start fitting wall units several points must be considered.

❏ Do your wall units have to meet up with a pantry or wall oven? If so, then your level line is best run from the top of these units.
Note: If you are planning to fix wall tiles between your worktop and underside of wall cabinets, the top row of tiles may need to be cut to fit.

❏ If there are no restrictions on the height of your wall cabinets, you would be wise to use your tile size as a guide to the height above the worktop level for fixing wall units. e.g. 4 courses of 100 x 100 mm tiles = 400 mm above. Allow 2 mm for each grouting gap, say total of 410 mm, or with 3 courses of 150 x 150 mm tiles, total would be 450 mm plus 8 mm grouting gap = 458 mm.

❏ As wall units need to be suspended from the wall, extra fixing points may be required. It is recommended that each cabinet is fixed both at the top and bottom of the back. Otherwise two fixings at the top will usually be sufficient.

Kickboards
Your kit kitchen will come with kickboards or baseboards. In most situations these will require scribing to the floor before fixing into position. Use

Above: A straightedge and spirit level are used to check walls for plumb and straightness
Right: The 3:4:5 method for checking walls for square

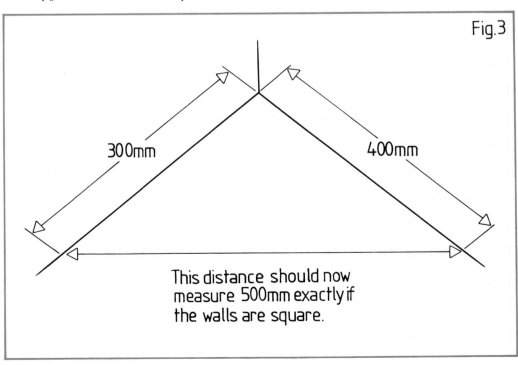

Fig.3

300mm

400mm

This distance should now measure 500mm exactly if the walls are square.

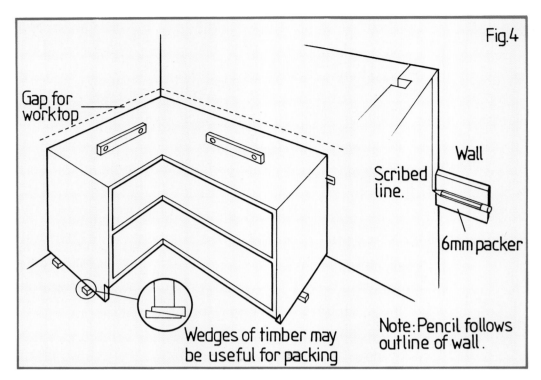

Fig.4

Gap for worktop

Wall

Scribed line.

6mm packer

Wedges of timber may be useful for packing

Note: Pencil follows outline of wall.

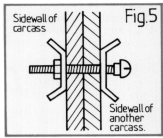

Fig.5

Sidewall of carcass

Sidewall of another carcass.

Left: Pack a corner cabinet with wedges until it is level
Above: A toggle bolt

the same methods as described in scribing floor units on page 28. If the kickboards are to be fitted to the legs, follow the manufacturer's instructions closely. Other types may be nailed on or glued with suitable wall-board adhesives. Mitre joints may also be required for external corners. These must be cut carefully. If mitre joints are not used you will have to finish off one edge.

Cutting and fitting appliances and sinks

Sinks Care should be taken at the planning stage to ensure that it is possible to install the sink you want in your kitchen. Note: You should check that all plumbing will fit into one cabinet. This may include the waste disposal unit or water purifier. Make sure they do not inhibit the opening and closing of doors or drawers.

Marking out: The cut required should be done carefully, allowing enough space for the taps selected, if no provision is made for them in the sink. Allow for overhangs.
Note: Check twice and cut once (exceptionally good advice). Avoid putting the sink over any worktop joints if at all possible, as this will create a weak spot which water can penetrate. Use a straightedge for marking as a

cutting guide. A jigsaw is the best cutting machine for this purpose. A small portable circular saw can be used but it must have fine, sharp teeth.
Fixing down: Use the clips provided by the manufacturer. Do not remove the foam strip that may be provided. After fixing, run a fine bead of silicone sealant around the sink. Allow it to set slightly before removing excess with a razor knife.

Cooktop (hob) and wall oven
Follow the same steps as for the sink except that no silicone sealant is required unless manufacturers specify it.

Score worktop with laminate knife to just below the coloured outer surface of the laminate

Note: Ensure that all plumbing and wiring meets the required regulations.

Doors and Drawers
Doors Fix the hinges to all your doors before you hang them. Do not drill any holes for handles until all doors have been hung and adjusted. Follow the manufacturers instructions as there are a wide variety in use today. Generally all modern hinges are 3-way adjusting: up and down, in and out and across and back.

1 A hinge plate may be required to be screw-fixed to the

inside of cabinets. Care should be taken to ensure that these are located correctly.

2 Hold the door against the cabinet in the open position and mark the position of the mounting plate.

3 Fix the door onto the mounting plates, tighten up and adjust. Now drill for handle holes if necessary.

Drawers These may come assembled or in kit form. Either way the main body of the drawer runner should be attached to the sides of the drawer unit. Assemble the drawer following the manufacturer's instructions. The drawer-fronts should already be attached. If not, this is the procedure:

1 With the bottom drawer in place, hold the bottom drawer-front against the drawer. Line the bottom edge

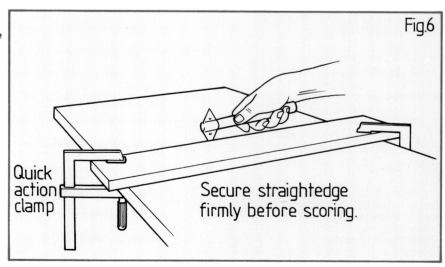

Fig.6

Quick action clamp

Secure straightedge firmly before scoring.

of the drawer-front up with the bottom edge of the adjoining doors and mark along the inside top edge of drawer.

2 Remove both drawer and drawer-front and attach temporarily with suitable nails.

3 Return drawer and adjust fit.

4 Insert next drawer. Place 1.5-2 mm packers on the top edge of bottom drawer-front. Sit the next drawer-front on top of packers and line up side gaps. Mark along the top edge. Repeat steps 2 and 3.

5 When all drawer-fronts have been attached and adjustments made, drill and screw-fix into place with four screws and fit handles if applicable.
Note: For appearance's sake,

all screws should be countersunk flush with all surfaces or a decorative cover cap should be used.

6 Any gaps may now be filled using a suitable gap filler (not a timber putty) or use quadrant mould pinned in place.

TIPSTRIP

Build two stands that will sit on the worktop to support the wall units at the correct height (see fig. 7).

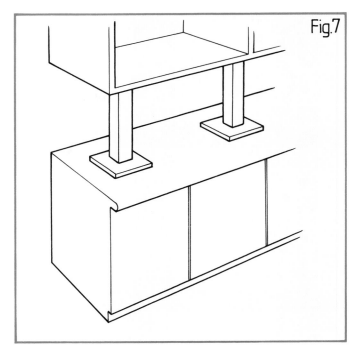

Fig. 7

Below: The impressive result of a few days work

Pro-Pak Kitchen, Mad Barry's

Cooking in a good light

Good light in a kitchen is essential from both a safety and a practical point of view. During the day, try to gain maximum benefit from natural light because it is easiest on the eyes.

While it's not always feasible to enlarge a window to make a dark kitchen brighter, there are other possibilities to consider; in a bungalow a skylight will greatly increase the general light level. One that opens or incorporates a vent is sensible for kitchen use. Other options include clear or opaque glass and blinds – the choice will depend on factors such as whether or not the skylight is in full sun or semi-shade. If you can't shed new light from above, look to the walls. Perhaps you can replace some of the masonry with glass bricks; they let light through without exposing you to public scrutiny.

If you can't alter what you have, remember that small windows should be kept clear of overgrowing vines on the outside and fussy curtains on the inside. If you need a covering to reduce glare or give privacy, choose a neat blind that folds or rolls up clear of the window panes. Light colours in the kitchen, and on any walls or fences immediately outside the window, will make the room appear brighter.

Once the sun goes down, of course, window size is irrelevant. You may need to cover it for privacy, to cut heat loss or simply to reduce distracting reflections. Any window covering in a kitchen should be easily cleaned –

cooking generates steam and grease and these trap dirt – so venetian blinds, wipeable roller blinds or washable curtains are ideal. Never have flowing curtains or paper blinds near the oven or cooktop (hob) because of the fire risk.

Light after dark

There are three main types of electric light for use in the kitchen. The first is the familiar tungsten bulb which can be used in hanging lamps, track lighting, semirecessed eyeball lights and underlights for wall cupboards. It gives a warm, yellow light which is pleasant, but its disadvantages are that it casts shadows and that the brighter the light the more heat it emits – a significant factor in a hot and steamy kitchen.

Fluorescent lighting overcomes the problems of shadow and heat and is also economical. But while it gives an excellent overall light level, it can be harsh. Food doesn't look its best under fluorescent lighting and many people find it tiring after a while. If your main source of light is fluorescent, specify that you want a natural, soft or daylight tube. Fluorescent lighting is not suitable for use with a dimmer switch, so it

should be avoided in dining areas. Small fluorescent tubes are ideal for installing under wall units, however.

Becoming more and more popular are halogen lights. These give a very pure light that is pleasant to work by. The

bulbs last longer than ordinary ones and are economical to run; they are available in a range of different angles of spread, making them suitable for both general and spot lighting. Of course, there have to be disadvantages, too. Halogen bulbs

Style Kitchens

Above right: The windows form one end of the kitchen and have been extended to the roof to give maximum light
Right: A stained glass window hides an ugly view while allowing natural light into the kitchen

are more expensive to buy in the first instance and they need careful handling – even traces of grease can affect their performance; because they are low-voltage, they need a transformer to step down the power. Some bulbs have their own built-in transformer, but this makes the bulb bulky. In a kitchen it is better to have one transformer for the entire lighting circuit – not a problem as long as the electrician knows what he's doing.

Light patches

When it comes to electric lighting, plan in advance. Installing wiring is easiest before the kitchen itself is actually built – otherwise be prepared for a lot of disruption. Every kitchen needs good general light, specific task lighting and, if the kitchen is also an eating area, atmospheric lighting.

General light usually comes from an overhead lamp. In a kitchen with a single, central light bulb, it is a simple matter to replace it with a fluorescent strip light or several spot lights on a track.

The spots should not be directed at the work surfaces (you'd forever be in your own shadow) but bounced off the ceilings and walls to give soft but good overall illumination. If you are building new or totally renovating, look at lights (either tungsten or halogen) recessed into the ceiling. Carefully positioned, these give good general and specific light – and

they don't collect dust the way pendant light fittings do!

For food preparation and cooking you need light where you are working. The best way to illuminate worktops is with small lights (either fluorescent or tungsten) fastened to the underside of the wall units as close to the front of the cupboard as possible. Small baffles or a pelmet in front of the tubes cut glare. Good light over a stove can be provided by an extractor hood that incorporates a lamp as well.

In a kitchen/dining room, the eating area needs its own lighting with, ideally, its own switch. A rise-and-fall pendant light over the table, operated by a dimmer switch, enables you to control the light level.

Top: A spot light set in brass
Above: A triangular-shaped shade can be suspended from the ceiling

Project 3

Cafe curtains

A scalloped heading is often used on cafe curtains. They look particularly good when hung from wooden curtain rings.

1 To work out the amount of fabric required, measure the width of the window and add 3 cm for seam allowance. Measure the length from the rod or track to the desired length of the curtains. Add 5 cm to the lower edge to allow for the hem and add 1.5 cm to the top edge for the scallop heading.

2 To make the scallop heading, first decide on the width of

MATERIALS	
fabric	curtain rings
scissors	tape measure
pins	
marking pen	
drinking glass	

TIME
1-2 hours

the scallops and the band between each scallop. As a general guide, scallops can be 8 cm wide with a 1.5 cm band in between, but you can alter this to suit the width of the window. Use a drinking glass and marking pen to draw the scallops onto a piece of cardboard to form a scallop template (fig. 1). Cut out the template and using a water-soluble pen, trace scallops 1.5 cm down from the top edge of the curtain.

3 Cut a fabric lining piece the width of the curtain and 6 cm longer than the base of the scallops. Stitch a narrow hem along the base of the lining piece. Pin and tack the lining to the top edge of the curtain, right sides of fabric facing. Stitch the two pieces together, following the scallop

lines (fig. 2). Trim, neaten and clip seam. Turn curtains to right sides and press.

4 Turn in side and base hems and stitch. Stitch curtain rings to the centre of each band piece (fig. 3). Curtains are now ready to hang on a rod or track.

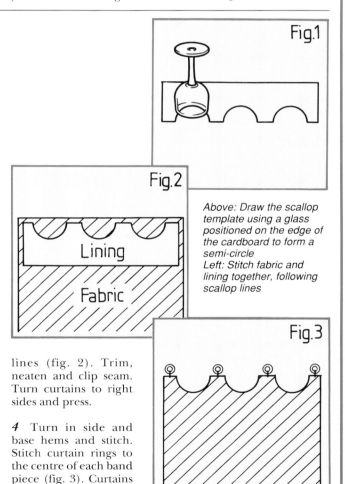

Above: Draw the scallop template using a glass positioned on the edge of the cardboard to form a semi-circle
Left: Stitch fabric and lining together, following scallop lines

Stitch curtain rings to centre of straight scallop edges

Selecting a suitable flooring from the dazzling array available can be a daunting task. Here we look at some practical considerations to help you make your choice.

THE RIGHT FLOOR

Choosing the flooring may be among the most difficult decisions you have to make in the design of your new kitchen. You'll be looking for something that's tough enough to stand up to spills, grease, damp and everyday wear and tear, that's not too hard underfoot and is non-slip, that will last a long time and not require too much maintenance, that looks attractive and, preferably, doesn't cost the earth. It's a tall order, and not all possibilities meet all those criteria; decide which ones are most important to you, and you'll be able to make an educated choice when you go out shopping for flooring.

One of the most important things you'll have to consider is whether the flooring of your choice is suitable for the construction of your house. You can lay almost any type of flooring on solid concrete, but you can't, for instance, put heavy quarry tiles on the average domestic timber-suspended floor without first seeking expert advice.

Your choice will be further narrowed down by the style of kitchen you want; if you're after a country look, rustic terracotta tiles may be the best choice, whereas if the effect you're aiming for is more sleek and modern, one of the new generation linoleums could be more suitable. Here we offer a general rundown of the most common types of flooring available, looking at their advantages, as well as possible disadvantages.

Vinyl sheeting and tiles

One of the most economical types of flooring, vinyl is also one of the most versatile. It comes in many different grades – from ultra-rigid tiles to the soft cushioned sheet flooring – giving you virtually any effect you desire. You can choose from patterns or plain colours or, for a fraction of the cost of the real thing, go for one of the look-alikes; marble, slate, tile or timber.

The main advantages of vinyl, apart from its price, are that it's hardwearing, easy on the feet, quiet, and resistant to water, grease and most domestic chemical products.

It's extremely important to lay vinyl correctly on an even surface to avoid lifting edges that eventually rip or bend. It can be laid on virtually any level, dry surface, except floorboards. To lay vinyl over timber, first put down an underlay of hardboard, smooth side up.

Vinyl's come a long way since those days when the very mention of it brought visions of hours of tedious waxing and polishing. Most of the new vinyls require very little maintenance; generally a daily sweep to remove grit, and washing once a week is sufficient. It's not strictly necessary to polish them, but their life will be prolonged if they are polished two or three times a year with a special vinyl polish. This is a simple job, easily done with a mop.

Linoleum

Linoleum's making a big comeback around the world, as manufacturers have shifted right away from the drab colours more often associated with school corridors and doctors' waiting rooms. Today, lino comes in a wide range of fabulous colours, from bright reds, blues and yellows to the more subtle greys and beiges, in plain or marbled effect.

It's an ideal flooring choice for the kitchen, being hardwearing, comfortable to walk on, usually forgiving to dropped china and glassware, handsome to look at and reasonably economical, being about the same price as mid to high-quality cushioned vinyl.

A 100 per cent natural product, lino is made of cork, resins, wood flour, mineral colours and with a backing of hessian. It's the cork in the lino that gives it its spring, which not only makes it easy to walk on, but also allows it to be laid on slightly uneven surfaces, without a hardboard underlay. However, a hardboard base is recommended if the lino is being laid on old irregular timber planks. Unlike vinyl, lino should be laid by a flooring expert; it is not a job for the do-it-yourselfer.

Maintenance of lino is simple: regular sweeping and mopping with an emulsion dressing. There is no need to use wax or polish. To get a high gloss finish, you can apply an acrylic sealer; manufacturers do not recommend it, however, if you're after low-maintenance flooring, as the sealer has to be stripped and re-applied every few years.

Unlike vinyl, lino is a homogeneous product,

Floor Country Floors

Above: Mexican tiles are
highlighted with a strong
coloured border
Right: Small colourful ceramic
tiles break the warm effect of
these terracotta tiles

**One of the most
important things
you'll have to
consider is whether
the flooring of your
choice is suitable
for the construction
of your house.
You can lay almost
any type of flooring
on solid concrete,
but seek advice
before laying heavy
quarry tiles on the
average domestic
timber floor.**

Floor and Jug Country Floors

meaning the colour goes right through from the top surface to the hessian base. Scratches and other surface damage, therefore, do not show up as easily. It's a tough product all round – with normal domestic use, it will last as long as you want it to. In fact, there have been instances of it being virtually as good as new after 80 years.

Daytile Cork, Armstrong Nylex

Rubber

Another option that's hardwearing, with excellent insulation and sound absorption qualities is rubber. Available in a number of fashionable colours, rubber tiles generally have either a round or square studded profile. They can be laid on a cement or hardboard base, and could be tackled quite easily by the enthusiastic do-it-yourselfer.

Rubber doesn't take much looking after – just regular vacuuming, and it

may be shined with a water-based polish to give a glossy surface.

Cork

Because of its elastic properties, cork makes an excellent kitchen flooring material. Its soft and springy surface is more likely to cushion the fall of glass than, say, ceramic tiles would. It's a good insulator, is tough, and easy to look after. Maintenance, apart from re-coating when necessary, consists only of washing with warm water and a mild detergent.

Part of the appeal of cork lies in its colourings – warm tones ranging from honey to deep brown, and also, with new liming techniques, soft greys – which complement many types of kitchen decor.

Cork tiles can be glued onto almost any level, dry, clean surface including steel-trowelled concrete,

although over timber floorboards an underlay of hardboard is required. After the tiles have been laid – a job which can be carried out by the amateur – they are sanded and given three or more coats of sealer. You need to wait 24 hours between each coat of sealer; therefore, care must be taken to make sure that dust particles don't get trapped in the cork.

Although cork is easy to maintain, it does have a few disadvantages. It can rot if water is trapped underneath it; strong, direct sunlight can fade it; the edges of the tiles are vulnerable to chipping, and it needs to be re-sealed every few years.

Parquet

Parquet flooring, a handsome choice for kitchens, comes in blocks or tiles, and is available in dozens of patterns and many different types of timbers. It is certainly not a low budget option – but actual price obviously depends on the timber used and

the pattern. It can be laid on any level, clean and dry surface, including concrete or timber. It's easy to look after; requiring only regular sweeping, and then re-sealing every few years.

Vinyl has come a long way since those days when the very mention of it brought visions of hours of tedious waxing and polishing. Most of the new vinyls require very little maintenance; generally a daily sweep to remove grit, and washing once a week is sufficient.

Left: Vinyl tiles can give many different effects – these resemble a cork floor
Below: Parquet flooring allows interesting patterned effects

Ware Collingwood Floors

The Slate People

TIPSTRIP

To create a feeling of space in a small kitchen, you should look at not only the layout of the room, but also at decorative aspects, including the flooring. Choose something plain and light-coloured – sheet vinyl, linoleum, cork, timber, ceramic or quarry tiles. It's best to avoid patterns, unless you opt for a fairly subtle effect, such as a classic chequerboard tile. As you're only having to cover a small space, perhaps this is your opportunity to lash out on a luxurious flooring option.

Slate

An expensive but beautiful flooring option, slate is available in a wide range of colours, from greeny-grey to black. It's very hardwearing and easy to care for, needing only a regular mopping with household detergent or washing soda, but it can be quite noisy, as well as slippery when wet. Slate is not as cold a material as you would expect, warming up to room temperature quite quickly, and retaining heat efficiently. Being non-porous, there is also little risk of it staining.

Slate tiles, which have either sawn edges or are guillotined to give a hand-cut appearance, can be laid on timber, concrete or a cement base, and is a simple DIY project.

Both slate and marble can be slippery, so think carefully about using them if you have small children.

Marble

Although wonderful to look at, marble is not the most practical material for kitchen floors, as it is slightly porous, easily scratched, and stained by things like wine, citrus juice, oils and vegetable dyes. If you are determined to use marble, seek expert advice as some types are more suitable than others.

To clean, wipe over with diluted dishwashing liquid, without allowing the floor to get too wet. Abrasive cleaners must not be used on marble, as they scratch. If the floor does become stained or badly scratched, seek professional advice.

Ceramic tiles

There's an almost unlimited range to choose from here – from large plain tiles in subtle tonings to highly patterned, brightly coloured ones in modern designs, plus any number in between. They can be slightly cold in the kitchen – you may need underfloor insulation to cope with those chilly winter mornings. Without sound-absorbing furnishings, they can also be noisy, and, of course, are unforgiving to dropped china and glassware. However, they are tough, waterproof, available in non-slip grades and impervious to most household liquids. For cleaning, you only have to mop over them with warm soapy water.

With the country and provincial looks being so fashionable today, terracotta tiles, especially quarry tiles, are very popular. Unsealed terracotta is generally unsuitable for kitchens, as it stains, but pre-sealed tiles are available, which are easier to look after.

Left: Slate comes in a wide range of colours
Below: Studded rubber floor tiles form a clean and practical floor surface

Studz, Kenbrock Floors

Project 4

Laying a vinyl tile floor

Vinyl tiles are an excellent surface for kitchen floors, easier to lay than sheet vinyl and easier to repair by replacing individual tiles.

To do the job properly it is essential that the floor underneath is perfectly flat, achievable only with concrete slabs that have been steel-trowelled or finished with self-levelling cement, or with rougher slabs and floorboards that have been covered with underlay sheets. This second option is more accessible to DIY enthusiasts.

Note: Manufacturers supply information sheets that cover all aspects of this kind of job.

STEP BY STEP

1 The underlay

Underlay sheets are most likely to be of either masonite or fibre-cement, the latter being easier to lay, immune to water damage and giving a better, more rigid surface.

Floorboards must be flat. If boards are badly warped the whole floor must be rough-sanded before the underlay can be fixed. Floor sanders can be hired and are worth the expense. Remove lumps from concrete with a cold chisel.

Start laying the sheets in a corner of the room, keeping sheet edges about 3 mm away from walls. Lay out all the sheets on the floor and cut where necessary before fixing any to the floor. Ensure that nailheads are flush with the surface of the sheets before laying the tiles. It may be necessary to sand the joints between the sheets if the floor beneath is really rough.

2 The tiles

When setting out, try to avoid tile edges falling within 80 mm of underlay joins. Avoid narrow pieces near walls and always use the cut edge against walls or cupboards rather than against other tiles. Use only the adhesive recommended by the tile manufacturer and follow instructions carefully.

3 The centre line

Use tiles laid loose to establish the longest perpendicular line through the room that will give an equal distance to the closest walls on either side. Use a chalk line or a tight string line suspended between two nails.

4 Beginning

Sweep the floor carefully. Loose-lay tiles along and out from the centre line (see fig. 1), establishing what size the border tiles will be. Any one of these centre tiles can be your first laid. Using a notched trowel to spread the adhesive, prepare an area equal to about six tiles along the centre line. Place the tiles as close to their proper position as possible to avoid having to slide them.

As each tile is laid, press it down with the palm of your hand and rub the surface firmly. You must assume that the tiles are cut perfectly square during manufacture so you should not allow any cracks to appear between them as they are laid. Immediately remove any adhesive which has spread on the floor or smeared the tiles.

Note: Boxes of tiles should be well mixed before the first one is laid because you cannot assume that the colour will be constant from box to box. Selecting boxes with the same batch number when purchasing tiles gives some insurance.

5 Cutting tiles

When cutting tiles around the edges, lay the tile to be cut over the adjacent tile, making sure the pattern is the right way up. Then lay another full tile over the top and push it hard against the wall. You will now have a thickness of three tiles. Using the top tile as a gauge, score the second tile with your trimming knife (see fig. 2). Remove the top tile and cut through the second tile and it will fit perfectly into the space. Repeat this process until all edge tiles are in place.

6 Finishing

Walk around for a while on the tiles or hire a roller, making sure that all adhesive is removed and that all tiles are sticking down well. Wait 24 hours before moving heavy items such as the fridge into place on your new floor.

MATERIALS
tiles
adhesive
underlay sheets
nails

TOOLS
knife
hammer
notched trowel
string or chalk line
disposable cloth
steel ruler
tape measure

TIME
1-2 days

Lay the tiles along and out from the centre line

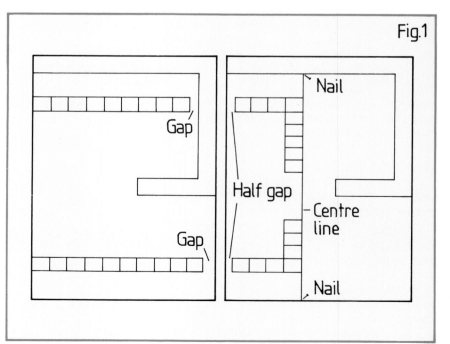

Fig.1

Gap

Gap

Nail

Half gap

Centre line

Nail

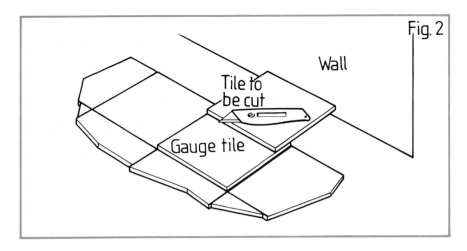

Fig. 2

Wall

Tile to be cut

Gauge tile

Left: A foolproof method of cutting tiles.
Below: Easy-to-lay vinyl tiles make a great surface for kitchen floors

Daytile Flint, Armstrong Nylex

Start with a well-designed kitchen; mix that with a carefully thought-out colour scheme and personal decorating touches, and the result will be an individual and interesting room that will be in keeping with the rest of the house.

COLOUR AND DECOR

While the working parts of the kitchen are vitally important, so too are the decorative aspects – you want to create a room that you feel happy working in. There's no point in having all the latest appliances and high technology if you're miserable every time you set foot in the kitchen. Think just as carefully about colour and the decorating of the room as you do about every other aspect. The beauty of decorating decisions is that few are final – if you get tired of the wall colour, it's a lot easier to change than, say, the oven or worktop. For this reason, you can be a little more adventurous with your decorating scheme, safe in the knowledge that if you discover you've made a terrible mistake it's not irrevocable.

As the actual bones of the kitchen – the cabinetry, flooring and appliances – are expensive, it's probably wise to exercise restraint in these areas. It's safer to be conservative in your choice of colours for these elements, reserving the more exciting tones for the less permanent features such as paintwork.

The first thing to do when you're thinking about colour in the kitchen is to decide whether you want your kitchen to have the same colours as used in adjacent rooms. If you do, your choice will be narrowed down enormously. If not, you will have a virtually open palette.

Then think about the effect you want to achieve. As a rule of thumb, if you want to create an intimate, cosy mood, you should choose warm tones such as reds and oranges, or even blues and greens containing a lot of yellow. If you're after a more sophisticated, cooler look, blues and greens are more suitable, or, again, reds and yellows with a great deal of blue. Even whites, greys, browns and blacks can seem either cool or warm depending on the amount of yellow or blue they contain.

Have a look at the quality of natural light in the room. Do you want to emphasise it, or not? Cool colours can tone down the heat of such light, while warm ones can intensify it.

Colour in the room can come from a variety of sources – paintwork, wallpaper, the splashback, fabric, prints, china – the

The beauty of decorating decisions is that few are final – if you get tired of the wall colour it's a lot easier to change than the oven or worktop.

Bright, adventurous colour can be used to great advantage in the kitchen

Kitchen Architecture

list goes on. The most obvious way to inject life into the room is with paint, and not just on the walls; have a look at the detailing of the room – windows, doors, picture rails and so on – and see if any of these can be picked out. Red might be too much for complete walls, but the odd touch on architraves or window frames may be just right. Similarly, brightly coloured cabinetry might be overwhelming, but drawer handles of that same colour can add a certain amount of pizzazz.

Be careful, if you do decide to emphasise certain features in the room, that you pick out the more attractive ones.

elements to avoid a bitty and confusing effect. Be as bold as you like with these trim colours.

In some kitchens, it is worth featuring certain structural elements. A case in point would be a window with deep sill. Choose a contrasting colour for the complete recessed area to emphasise this attractive architectural feature. The window frame itself can be painted in another shade. The sill can then be used as a shelf for cookery books, or for displaying treasured objects. If light is not a consideration in the room, extra shelves could be installed into the recess, and these could be used for display or storage.

Tablemats, napkins and teatowels, can create a single, bold colour in an otherwise monochromatic scheme. Have several sets to suit your moods.

scheme of the room – you could select something that coordinates with your colour scheme or provides contrast.

Cups and Saucers The Bay Tree

For instance, the doors, cornices and skirting boards may be worth painting in a contrasting colour, but the pipes and pillars may be decidedly unappealing. When picking out details, it is probably best to err on the side of conservatism; highlight only one or two

Even with an all-white kitchen it's possible to add a little bit of colour – one or two drawers can be fronted with a different coloured laminate, as, too, can the splashback and perhaps a small area of worktop. When you tire of these colours it's not a major job to update them.

To create a room with appeal and individuality, group together well-loved and carefully chosen objects that share a common theme. These could be anything from plates, boxes and kitchen utensils to baskets and glassware. Decorative plates can look wonderful hung on the wall; basketware sitting on top of the kitchen cabinets is equally appealing. For a completely individual look, start collecting something unusual; how about framed orange wrappers; jelly moulds or old kettles?

Artwork need not be reserved for the living areas of the house; framed posters, children's artwork, botanical prints or lithographs can look terrific on a kitchen wall. Choose the frames and mountings carefully to tie in with the decorating

Above: China and other kitchen crockery or accessories can be used to coordinate with the colour scheme
Left: Inject colour into the kitchen with pictures or prints
Right: Wallpaper is an unusual but interesting feature which can add colour and pattern to a kitchen

Practicalities

Paint

❑ **Acrylic paint:** You use water to wash your brushes with this type of paint. It's longer lasting than oil-based gloss paint, as it's not as brittle and therefore less likely to flake or peel. Water resistant and tough, it's easy to use and suitable for wall and ceiling areas. Flat finishes are not recommended for hard-working areas in the kitchen; the glossier finishes are a lot more dirt-resistant and easier to clean.

❑ **Oil-based gloss paint:** With this type of paint, you use turps (white spirit) to clean your brushes. It's recommended where a glossy, hardwearing surface is required. Kitchen cupboards, skirting boards and doors are best painted in gloss. Make sure you sand carefully between coats for a long-lasting and smooth finish.

Always use washable paint in the kitchen.

Try some of the fashionable paint techniques like spongeing, rag rolling and stencilling to give your kitchen an individual look. You don't have to use these techniques over the entire walls – a window frame, archway or door may be enough.

TIPSTRIP

False paint finishes – dragging, ragging and marbling – can be used to liven up virtually anything in the kitchen from walls, skirting boards and cupboard doors to the telephone and the freezer. Practice, but not great artistic skill, is all that is required. There are dozens of books available complete with step-by-step instructions; look in your local library or bookshop.

Gloss paints can give new life to existing tiles. Wash the tiles down thoroughly with soap and water, and leave for 24 hours. To remove all traces of grease, wipe down with methylated spirits and then paint. One coat will be sufficient, and there is no need to use undercoat. Gloss paint, however, can show up every irregularity in plasterwork – you may opt for a softer sheen.

Before committing yourself to a particular colour in the kitchen, buy sample pots of paint and brush small patches onto different parts of the wall (the lightest and darkest areas). Live with them for a while before making your final decision.

Wall coverings

Always use a wallpaper paste with a built-in fungicide.

Washable wallpapers are inexpensive and are coated with a thin plastic film. They can be wiped over but are not tough enough to be scrubbed. They are not recommended for heavy duty areas; here, the more durable and more expensive ranges in which the design is actually printed onto a layer of vinyl are more suitable.

Interesting objects like these pastry cutters can add a unique decorative touch

Pastry Cutters The Bay Tree

Nairn Decor

Try some of the fashionable paint techniques like rag rolling and stencilling to give your kitchen an individual look.

Left: Kitchen utensils have been chosen to complement the wall colours
Below: A wonderful tile mural can give an artistic and vibrant touch to a kitchen

Tile Mural Jenny Orchard

Timber panelling

Tongue-and-groove softwood panelling is ideal for covering ugly plumbing or uneven walls. It can be stained or varnished or, for a softer look, painted to match the decor.

In a country-style kitchen, a dado of timber panelling can be installed, with the wall above painted or papered. As there is a gap between the wall and timber panelling, it is a good choice for the kitchen which has condensation problems.

Cork tiles

They retain heat and absorb moisture so are a sensible choice for rooms that are either cold, or suffering from condensation problems.

Use presealed tiles, or give unsealed tiles two coats of polyurethane varnish after installation.

Bricks

If you have a wall of exposed brickwork, seal it with a masonry stabiliser to prevent it absorbing grease and stains.

Tiles

Tiles are the toughest form of wallcovering. There is a huge range available, from comercially produced tiles to hand-painted ones which you can buy singly and use as a feature. On areas prone to constant splashing, such as behind the sink, use waterproof and stain-resistant grout.

A drawback of tiles is that they are difficult to remove once in place, so choose carefully.

Project 5

Stencilling

A stencilled frieze on your kitchen wall is a lovely and very individual decorative touch.

You can also stencil a border or motif on your kitchen cupboards, the backs of wooden chairs or on a painted table.

STEP BY STEP

1 Draw your design onto a sheet of acrylic film or a piece of manila cardboard using a felt-tipped pen. If using cardboard first strengthen it by liberally applying a mixture of 50 per cent linseed oil and 50 per cent turpentine (white spirit) to both sides of the board. Allow it to soak in and then rub off excess moisture with a soft cloth.

Carefully cut out the stencil with a sharp craft knife or a surgical scalpel.

2 Using masking tape, fasten the stencil in position. Make sure the edges of the stencil are straight, and the design a uniform distance in from the edges so that you can simply butt the stencil up to the cornice, worktop or door frame when positioning it.

If your frieze is to go around corners, take measurements first to establish where a corner will occur in the pattern. Small positional adjustments at the

start may prevent difficult or awkward painting at the corner. Some designs will simply slide around the corner with no visible disruption to their continuity – others are clearly unbalanced as they turn. Sometimes you can stop the stencil just slightly short of the corner and simply take some single design element and place it right in the corner, continuing the stencil again on the other side.

3 Pour a little acrylic or emulsion paint into a saucer. Do not add any water, and be sure your brush is dry. Using a dabbing movement, dip the brush into the paint, dabbing off any excess. It may be necessary to paint a few strokes first, on spare fabric or kitchen towels to make sure the brush holds only a minimum of paint. Too much paint on the brush will seep under the stencil edges and cause indistinct outlines.

Start to fill in the stencil design with paint using a dabbing movement. Do not stroke the brush. Don't try to make the paint coverage entirely even. Part of the charm of stencilling is that paint shades

and definition will inevitably differ from motif to motif. Once the paint is almost dry remove stencil carefully. It is important not to allow excess paint to build up on the cut stencil, so either wipe over or wash the stencil between uses. Dry paint build-up can distort the outlines of the stencil and encourage paint to seep in and blur the edges.

4 Once the first motif is finished and the paint is almost dry, you may position the stencil again to continue the border pattern. Acrylic paint dries very quickly (2-3 minutes). This repositioning is easy with acrylic sheeting because it's transparent. If you're using manila cardboard, notch the edges of it and use the notches as a repositioning guide.

If you have blurred the edge of an outline, quick attention will solve the problem. Usually a water-dampened cotton bud can be used to wipe this edge or to fix any other small mistake. Touch-ups with a fine paintbrush can be useful for redefining small areas you have missed or that are indistinct.

Dab the paint onto the stencil, making sure you don't overload the paintbrush

Wait until the first stencil is almost dry before you position the next one

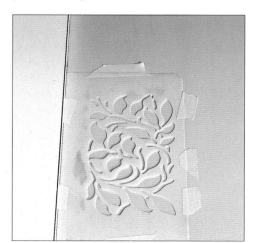
Tape the stencil in position with masking tape. Make sure the edges are straight

MATERIALS

acrylic or emulsion paint
clear acrylic film or manila cardboard
linseed oil and turpentine (white spirit)

TOOLS

flat-topped brush
craft knife or surgical scalpel
cloth

TIME

1 day

The navy-blue kitchen cupboard fronts are softened by pale coffee walls, and then stylishly balanced with a navy stencil of traditional willow leaves. The contrast in textures is extended with the displayed collection of old and new willow cane baskets

The requirements of a worktop are that it should be tough enough to cope with all sorts of attack, yet sufficiently good-looking to be a design element in the kitchen.

WORK SURFACES

The worktop is probably the most hardworking part of the whole kitchen; over the years it has to stand up to all sorts of abuse from knives, hot saucepans, water, kitchen chemicals and certain foods.

Some materials wear better than others or are relatively easy to repair; think about these things when you're deciding what to use for your worktop. You should also consider what maintenance will be required, and how often; whether splashback edges and corners can be well sealed; if you have a long worktop, how many joints there will be; and then, look at the relative prices of the different materials. These are the practical considerations – after that it's a matter of making your decision purely on aesthetic grounds.

Laminates

The most economical worktop material, laminate is also one of the most practical. It comes in an extraordinary array of colours, designs and textures from subtle and sophisticated to zany and eye-catching; one type or another is certain to be suitable for your kitchen, whether you want a country look or are more into hi-tech. Some of the newer designs also offer quite realistic, and much cheaper, alternatives to expensive timber, marble and granite.

There are different types of laminate – the standard variety, which is a thin coloured layer stuck down to a particle (chip) board or plywood base, and, a more recent development, solid laminates which allow for softer curved edges and eliminate the black edging joins seen in the conventional laminates. The solid variety also makes scratches and chips harder to see.

Horizontal-grade laminates are reasonably hardy, and can withstand a reasonable amount of abuse, but it's important to use heatproof mats to avoid buckling and scorching, and chopping boards to avoid scratching. Prolonged exposure to water may cause warping. If looked after carefully, they have a long life, but once damaged, they're very difficult to repair.

Laminates are easy to maintain – they resist grease and stains, and clean up well with mild household detergents and warm water.

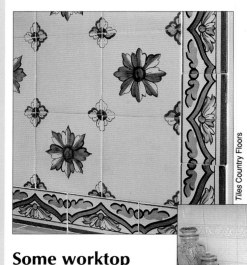

Tiles Country Floors

Some worktop materials wear better than others, or are relatively easy to repair.

Corotone, Parbury's

Left: Hand-painted tiles are one of the stunning choices available. Tiles can be used for splashbacks and as a workbench surface
Below: This man-made solid surface, similar to Corian®, extends along the worktop and includes a sink made from the same material

Right: Laminate surfaces now come with softly curved edges in a wide range of colours

Laminex Industries

Corian®

Corian is the registered trade mark for a man-made worktop material which looks like marble but is much tougher than the real thing, being highly resistant to heat and stains. It can be cleaned with abrasive cleaners and scourers, and has the added advantage that if scratches do occur, they are easily sanded or scoured away. Corian can be worked like timber, and such features as rounded edges, non-drip edges and juice grooves are often incorporated into the worktop design. It is certainly not a budget option.

Avonite®

This is another manufactured composite material which has the appearance of granite, can be worked to form almost invisible joins and comes in about a dozen colours. As with Corian, it's virtually maintenance-free, and is resistant to staining and heat. Any scratches that do occur can be removed with light sanding.

Timber

While undoubtedly an attractive material, timber, in solid planks, glue-laminated or recycled forms, is not always the most sensible choice for worktops. It can deteriorate and lose colour after constant wear from hot and cold liquids, eventually exposing the grain. The only thing to do then is to strip the timber back, sand it and reseal it. Hot saucepans and timber worktops do not make a good combination, and neither do chopping knives and timber. If it is washed down too often with detergents, it can lose its natural oils and split.

Having said all that, timber will acquire a rich patina over time and you may feel the scratches, nicks and stains add character rather than look unattractive.

However, if the imperfections would annoy you, and you're determined to have a timber kitchen, your best bet would be to use either one of the plastic laminate timber look-alikes, or restrict the use of timber to shelves and cupboard doors.

Stainless steel

Much more popular for commercial than domestic use, stainless steel is, nevertheless, making inroads into the home kitchen. First seen as sinks and draining boards, it's now often used to form complete worktops. It's hygienic, easy to look after (as long as you don't scratch it with scourers or abrasive powders), doesn't stain and is impervious to heat. On the down side, though, it can be noisy; insulation boards glued to the underside of the worktop can help reduce clatter. It is also expensive, but does look especially good with other industrial-type components such as commercial ovens and wire mesh shelves.

Marble

An expensive choice, marble is not altogether practical as a worktop. It's slightly porous, and therefore stains easily, with the biggest culprits being some reasonably common foodstuffs such as certain vegetable dyes, wine and citrus juices. Being quite a soft material, it also scratches fairly easily.

Some types of marble are less porous than others, so if you are determined to use it in your kitchen, it is worth seeking expert advice before you decide on the variety. For those who enjoy baking, marble provides a naturally cool surface for pastrymaking; however, a marble inset may provide a more practical alternative than surfacing the whole worktop in the material.

Soap and water can be used to clean marble; abrasive cleaners are unsuitable as they scratch. Severe stains can be polished out by professionals, and the use of commercial sealers will prevent some staining.

Granite comes in colours from grey and green to blue, black and red

Kitchen Country Form

Plate, Cups and Saucers The Bay Tree

Above: Wood is an attractive and durable work surface
Left: This man-made work surface resembles granite but is less expensive

Granite

This would have to be the ultimate worktop choice, if budget concerns were not taken into consideration. It's virtually indestructible, impervious to heat and liquids, scratch and chip-resistant, and non-porous. It's available in fabulous colours from greys and greens through reds and blues to black, and comes with square, bevelled or bullnosed edges. One thing you have to be careful about, though, is that granite is a very hard material, and unforgiving to dropped china and glassware. When it's first installed you have to adjust the force with which you put down the china to avoid chips or breaks.

Ceramic tiles

With the increased choice of worktop materials over the years, ceramic tiles are

Laminate is the most economical and practical worktop material.

losing their popularity for this particular job. That's probably just as well, as they are not particularly suitable. The grouting, unless epoxy, can very quickly become discoloured and is difficult to clean; the tiles themselves are noisy, and can crack if hot saucepans are put onto them. They are also quite fragile, and can chip or break if anything heavy is dropped onto them. Highly glossed tiles tend to show wear fairly quickly, too. All in all, it's probably sensible to restrict tiles to floors and splashbacks.

Project 6

Tiling a kitchen wall

Tiles still make the best wall surface between kitchen worktops and overhead cupboards.

They are easy to clean and make a watertight seal between walls and worktops as well as providing an opportunity for colour and decoration.

The most important thing to remember when tiling is to think it all out carefully before beginning. A careful sketch based on laying the tiles out on the worktop is worth the time it takes and will almost certainly reduce the likelihood of mistakes that might not become obvious until towards the end of the job.

STEP BY STEP

1 If you don't have a smooth rendered or plaster wall to start with you'll have to fit 6 mm fibre cement sheeting (e.g. Masterboard) as a flat base to which the tiles will be fixed. Nail or screw the sheets into place with 2-3 mm gaps between them to allow for movement.

2 Using a spirit level establish whether your worktops are level. If not, the first row of tiles

you fit will have to be one tile up from the lowest point of the worktop and the bottom row will have to be cut to fit later.

3 Draw a level line around the walls as the baseline for your first row of complete tiles. A chalk line may be best for this if a window has to be negotiated. Pin a batten along this line. The first row of tiles will rest on it (see fig. 1).

4 Lay your tiles out along the batten using matchsticks or bought plastic tile spacers between them to allow for the grout. Where this is awkward, mark out tiles plus joint widths along a length of batten and use this as a measuring stick. Choose the most inconspicuous spot for the inevitable cut tiles. This is often in a corner. Now decide on where to place your picture or feature tiles (see fig. 2).

5 Remember that it is much easier to cut a tile towards the

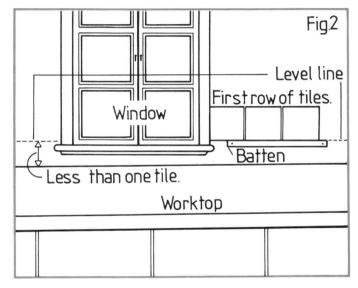

Fig.1

Half tile · Half tile · Full tile · Full tile · Battens · Level line · Worktop

Fig.2

Level line · First row of tiles. · Window · Batten · Less than one tile. · Worktop

middle than to trim off a small piece. Remember also that you must tile along a level line regardless of whether the verticals and horizontals of your worktops, cupboards and windows are true.

6 Now that you have it all worked out, start applying your adhesive with a notched trowel, about one square metre at a time. Use matchsticks or tile spacers and never, under any circumstances, allow the gaps to vary as you place the tiles.

Start at the centre and work outwards, leaving all cut tiles to the end. Bed the tiles into the adhesive firmly, sliding them back and forth a little and tapping them with your fist or a piece of wood. Use a straight-

edge to ensure that they are bedding evenly. Ensure that the adhesive does not come up between the tiles. Wipe it out, and off the face of the tiles with a damp cloth as you go.

Leave the battens and matchsticks, if used, in place for at least 12 hours as the adhesive takes a while to gain full strength.

7 Now for cutting in the odd-shaped tiles. When marking, hold a full tile over the last tile laid in the row. Butt the tile to be cut against the wall and under the tile you are holding while you mark the cut with a fibre-tip pen, allowing for grout.

8 A tile-cutting device, hired cheaply, is the best way to go. In

MATERIALS	TIME
tiles of your choice fibre cement sheeting grout tile adhesive stud adhesive clouts or countersunk screws and plugs	Normally 2-3 days. Don't rush it

TOOLS
notched tiler's trowel tile cutter, wheel and handle type (hired) tungsten-tipped tile cutter tile file cloth, sponges and bucket spirit level drill and high quality masonry bit

the end the number of tiles saved from breakage will almost certainly make for a cheaper, less frustrating job. Place the tile in the machine face up, line up your marks with the scribing wheel, scribe and press down on the handle. The tile should snap cleanly along the scribed line. Do not try to cut off less than 40-50 mm. Lay as you cut them.

9 Fitting around tap holes and power outlets can mean the loss of a few tiles. If possible, avoid having to cut a complete hole in a tile. Instead, lay your tiles out so that you cut sections out of three or four tiles. Cut a bigger hole or bite out of the tile than you need but not so big that the tap or powerpoint cover-plates will not cover it. Use a tungsten car-

bide-tipped tile cutter, score the marked line and take it out piece by piece with tile pincers. Alternatively, use a hacksaw with a tile cutting blade. A complete hole in a single tile can be achieved by drilling a starting hole with a masonry drill and cutting out with a tile-cutting blade. Smooth the cut edges with a tile file.

10 Grouting should not begin for at least 24 hours after your last tile was laid. Mix the grout as per the instructions on the pack. If colouring the grout add a small amount of oxide at a time until you reach the desired colour, or use precoloured grout. Apply the grout by hand (use rubber gloves) or with a rubber-bladed grout applicator. Fill all joints to overflowing and wipe off excess with a damp sponge. Use silicone sealant or a proprietary sealing strip on the joint between the wall and the worktop.

11 When the surface is dry remove the excess grout. Dust with a clean polishing cloth.

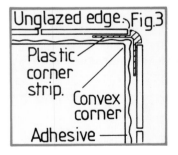

Ceramic tiles are not only the most hardwearing surface for the area between your worktop and cupboards, but also can be your kitchen's focal point

Tiles Country Floors *Kitchen Country Form*

Cat door

A cat door not only benefits the cat, it brings peace of mind to the cat owner.

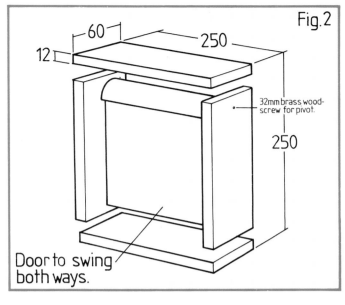

Fig.2

60 | 250

12

250

32mm brass wood-screw for pivot.

Door to swing both ways.

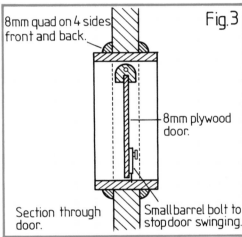

Fig.3

8mm quad on 4 sides front and back.

8mm plywood door.

Section through door.

Small barrel bolt to stop door swinging.

The hole should be cut in the bottom of the door on the lock-side so any framing will not interfere with the normal door operation. The door needs to be approximately 250 x 250 mm or smaller, depending on the size of your cat.

The door shown in the drawings can be locked for security, if required, or to simply stop a draught. Make sure that the cat door is positioned far enough away from the door lock, so that it cannot be reached by long-armed bandits! In any case, don't leave the key in the lock.

STEP BY STEP

1 Remove door, mark out the opening (250 x 250 mm) and cut out. The opening should be approximately 100 mm from the edge of the door. Take care not to damage the facing of the door. Use a fine bladed jigsaw or pad saw.

2 Make up the cat door frame from 60 x 12 mm DAR (PAR) timber to outside dimensions of 250 x 250 mm.

3 Make up the door from 8 mm plywood with a timber trimmer on top. Create an 8 mm slot in the trimmer with saw and chisel or an electric router. Round off the top with a plane and sandpaper. Leave 2 mm clearance around the door and pivot it on 32 mm brass wood screws. Make holes in the frame with clearance to allow the door to swing freely.

4 Insert the frame and door as an assembly into the pre-cut hole in the back door. Secure it to the door with 8 mm quadrant on both sides (see fig. 3). Fit lock if required.

5 Paint with a good oil-based primer then one or two coats of gloss.

Fig.1

MATERIALS
timber
PVA adhesive
nails
sandpaper
paint
lock, optional

TOOLS
electric drill
jigsaw or pad saw
hammer
chisel or electric router
plane
tape and pencil

TIME
4 hours

Sinks and taps

Not long ago, sinks and taps were the most boring things in the kitchen. Now they are among the most colourful.

Sinks and taps can add a touch of glamour and good looks to every kitchen. Indeed, the variety of styles and finishes now available calls for careful selection.

Sinks

Finance and space, for most people, are unalterable influences on the choice but, working within those parameters, you should also consider how you will use the sink.

Probably the most important factor is whether or not you have a dishwasher. If you do not, the prime purpose of the sink should be to make the task of washing up as easy as possible. Ideally, you should have twin bowls and double draining boards: this allows a natural work flow of stacking dirty dishes, washing, rinsing and draining. If space limits you to a one-and-a-half bowl style, take into account whether you like to work from left to right or the other way round. The larger bowl should be convenient for washing, and should be a minimum of about 17.5 cm deep and wide enough to take your biggest baking dish, the grill pan, oven shelves or anything else that may need long soaking.

It is best to avoid round sinks – it's surprising how many kitchen items don't

fit into them – and any without an integral draining board, as you will inevitably end up with small puddles of water lying on the worktop.

If you do have a dishwasher, or if space is very limited, you can look at the more compact styles, with smaller bowls and one or no draining board. The more sophisticated models make up for their lack in size in ingenuity: accessories that can be brought out as required include chopping boards, cutlery holders and plate racks that fit over the bowl, and separate draining boards. Other space-saving designs are corner sinks, which have the draining boards and bowls at right angles. They make good use of often 'dead' areas without encroaching on precious work surfaces. Well worth considering, whether or not you have limited space, is an allowance for a waste disposer.

A good setting

Virtually all compact designs and some larger sinks are designed to be set into the worktop. This allows flexibility as far as positioning goes: the hole can be cut anywhere along the worktop as long as there is sufficient room underneath for the sink bowls. Sit-on designs, supported by a unit of the same length, have the same depth as the worktop. Check that there is a watertight seal between the edge of the sink and the adjacent worktops.

Sink Clark

Sink Omega-Smeg

Material matters

As far as material goes, stainless steel still holds the number one position for durability and ease of cleaning. Enamelled and china sinks give you the opportunity of introducing colour but, although they have improved over the years, they are not a wise choice if you wash up by hand as they can chip. Brass looks charming in a traditional setting; it is durable and fairly easy to clean with a cream cleaner or brass polish.

Over the last decade or so, several manufacturers have developed composites which offer, at a price, considerable advantages. Not only are they extremely tough, resisting scratches, knocks, stains and heat, they are also much quieter, greatly reducing the clatter of pots and pans. They are available in a number of styles and different colours.

Top: A corner sink allows more room for dishes and maximises space
Above: Stainless steel is a popular choice for sinks

Tap lines

Like sinks, taps have danced their way into the nineties. Those immovable spouts fitted with coloured rubber nozzles are, thank goodness, things of the past. So too, are dripping taps. Improved technology – a ceramic disc instead of a washer – has put an end to drips for good. Because the discs are much longer lasting than washers, that tedious task of changing washers is destined to become a distant memory.

And there are other follow-on advantages: it's goodbye to ugly and immovable mineral stains on sinks and, of course, to a colossal waste of water. Quite apart from the environmental considerations, a dripping tap could cost you dear in areas where water use is metered. The new discs mean that a quarter turn of the handle is all that is needed to stop the flow, but tap designers have worked out ways to make water control even easier. Ergonomic single-lever designs mean that even the stickiest hands have no difficulty at all in turning the water on and off, or adjusting the temperature.

The two-handle, single-spout mixer-tap design is still appropriate in a traditional kitchen setting, but the single-lever designs win hands down for ease of use. They are operated by the lightest touch – even the nudge of an elbow if your hands are full or filthy – a fact that is appreciated by the elderly and disabled.

It's not just performance that has changed. Some taps have such sleek lines that they almost enter the art category; others are available in a positive rainbow of colours to complement or brighten any decorative scheme. Finishes available include numerous coloured epoxies, chrome, brass and gold. The last sounds like the ultimate extravagance and, of course, it is very expensive but

it is gradually gaining preference over brass because it is less likely to corrode.

At the other end of the price range, it is possible to change the handles on many of the less expensive tap designs: an old-fashioned tap that still functions well can be given a more modern look or a splash of colour with a very simple do-it-yourself project. You don't even have to turn the water off at the mains!

Whatever style you choose, it should be compatible with the sink in terms of finish, colour and function. The spout should swivel easily and be high enough for you fill a tall vase without tilting it. Don't be

wooed by an aesthetically beautiful tap if the handles are hard to control. Gimmicks are best avoided but extras that have proved their worth are brush and spray attachments and detergent dispensers. Along with the dozens of styles and colours there is, of course, an equal range of prices. Good taps are not cheap. If you are renovating your kitchen, don't treat taps as an afterthought. Choose the type you want and make allowances when you plan your budget. Buy the best you can afford – you will never regret investing in a good quality tap – but check, especially if it is an imported model, that it complies with your local water

board regulations. New taps don't always suit old plumbing systems either. If in doubt, ask the advice of a plumber.

Don't treat taps as an afterthought. Choose the type you want and make allowances when you plan your budget. Buy the best you can afford – you will never regret it.

Donson

Above: The gold sink set – a combination of classic styling and modern technology
Below: Chrome and white kitchen mixer. A mixer is the most convenient tap for the kitchen

Above: A streamlined chrome mixer tap, incorporating a watertight ceramic disc cartridge
Below: White kitchen mixer with a single lever which can be operated with the touch of an elbow

Argent Australia

The kitchen outlook

Standing at the sink, up to the elbows in dirty dishes, is a lot less painful if you are gazing at a landscaped garden or beautiful view.

No one would pretend that washing up is fun, but, if you really do have to stand up to the elbows in dirty dishes, the whole exercise would be a lot less painful if you were gazing at a beautiful view or landscaped garden. Unfortunately though, while planning can take care of making the interior of your kitchen as attractive and functional as possible, it's impossible to conjure up a fabulous panorama if you don't happen to have one at your back door.

However, in almost every case, you can make your kitchen outlook more pleasant; one that will add appeal to the whole room.

If you happen to look onto a brick wall, don't despair – that's easy to improve upon. To bring more light into the kitchen, and brighten up that dreary brickwork, consider painting it a colour that will coordinate with your interior decorating scheme. Use weatherproof paint for a long-lasting finish. If you really want to fantasise as you're slaving over the dishes, and you're artistically inclined, you could paint a trompe l'oeil mural outside the window. For starters – a fabulous beach scene, complete with crashing waves and sunbathers; or how about an alpine scene with snow-capped peaks; or a panorama across the Tuscan hills to a superb palazzo? There's no harm in dreaming!

For something a little more down to earth, look for metal pot rings, which you should be able to find in your local nursery. These are installed into the wall, and terracotta pots sit in them. An alternative would be wall-mounted terracotta plant holders. Grow herbs or, for a splash of colour, geraniums or annuals such as pansies. Likewise, a window box installed under the kitchen window can add a lively touch to an otherwise drab scene, or even a practical touch – keeping herbs literally close at hand. If you decide to grow flowers, find varieties that will give year-round colour.

Lattice or trelliswork attached to fences can give privacy as well as improve your outlook. Paint or stain it to suit, and then either leave it as is, or grow a climbing plant over it. Check with your local nursery to find the best plant for the position; choose from a flowering one, such as jasmine or one of the climbing roses, or a non-flowering variety, such as an ornamental grape, creeping fig or a variety of ivy.

If none of the above solutions is suitable for your particular problem view, you can always solve it from the inside. Consider venetian blinds – they can be tilted to get rid of offensive sights without blocking out the light completely, or you could invest in a translucent scenic roller blind.

Full-length windows take advantage of a fabulous panorama

Kitchen Country Form Egg basket and Teatowel The Bay Tree

Project 8

Window box

A simple wooden window box on your kitchen windowsill, filled with flowers or herbs, is the easiest way to improve your kitchen outlook.

You can fill the window box with soil or use it to hold plastic pots or a plastic trough. The size you make it should be determined by the size and type of window for which it is built. For a brick window it should fit snugly between the brickwork of the window opening, and for a timber house it should be the width of the window plus the exterior architraves.

STEP BY STEP

1 Choose your material. Pine is cheapest but tends to warp with the weather. Maple is better but cedar is the best. It is also the most expensive. Depth of the box should be determined as a pleasing proportion of the overall window size. About 200 mm is typical. Buy enough timber (200 x 25 mm DAR/PAR) for two sides, front, back and a bottom but check the timber as you buy it, rejecting any pieces that are not straight and true.

2 Measure and cut the pieces as in fig. 1, remembering that the nominal size of the timber is greater than what you will actually have in your hand. Note: If you are using only one size of timber, say 200 x 25 mm, then the front-to-back dimension of the box will be equal to the width of the timber plus two thicknesses for the front and back. The bottom, nailed on all sides, will sit snugly within the frame.

3 The rebate joint. The front piece needs to have a step chiselled out of each end for both strength and appearance. In this way no endgrain is visible from the outside. Across each end of the front piece, scribe a line at a distance from the end equal to the thickness of the timber, and another one about one-third of the way in on the endgrain (see fig. 2).

Using a mitre box or similar, cut across the grain about two-thirds of the way through the timber, making sure that both ends are cut to the same depth. Cut the side pieces last, as they will determine the overall width of the box, regardless of what depth you make the rebate. Carefully cut for the rebate with a saw and chisel at the step, using a 25 mm chisel.

4 The back needs only to be butt-jointed so the length of it will be the same as the front. The bottom should be the width of the timber to avoid a long cut, and as long as the overall length of the box, less two thicknesses for the sides. The sides should be cut last to ensure a good fit against the front and back.

5 Now the box is ready to assemble, but first the timber should be sealed with a synthetic preservative. Nail through the sides into the front at the rebate joints and then to the bottom, using rustproof nails. Also nail the front and the back to the bottom. Waterproof adhesive should be used on all joints for strength. Drill a number of holes in the bottom, towards the front, and seal the exposed timber with synthetic preservative.

6 If the sill is not wide enough to support the box, braces may be needed. Galvanised metal L-shaped braces may be used or simple timber ones can be easily made (see fig. 3).

7 To install, drill through the sides into the edge of the brickwork on both sides of the window opening with a masonry drill. Hammer the plastic wall-plugs into the brickwork, then screw through the sides into the plug. Repeat the technique to fix the braces. If installing in a timber-framed house, fixing is done by screwing the sides of the box into the edge of the window frame. Braces in this case must line up with the studs in the wall.

Finish with a coat of paint or stain.

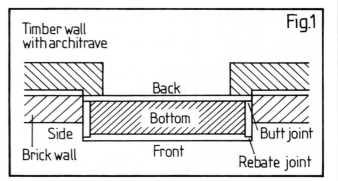

Fig.1

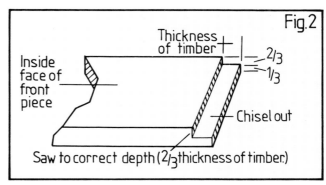

Fig.2

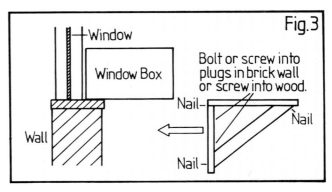

Fig.3

MATERIALS		TOOLS	
timber	wall-plugs	hammer	chisels
nails	braces	handsaw	level
screws		square	hand plane
waterproof adhesive		nail punch	paintbrush
timber preservative or		screwdriver	
waterproofer		tape measure	
		hammer drill and bit	
TIME			
4 hours			

Bringing the outdoors in

Eating outside is one of the great pleasures of life. A simple lunch achieves cordon bleu status if served in the fresh air, and there is no more enjoyable way of passing a summer evening than a leisurely dinner outdoors.

Even in a small garden it is worth setting aside an area for a table and chairs. Ideally your spot should be sheltered from the wind; it should catch the winter sun, but offer shade in the hot months. No, you can't change the course of the sun, but you can grow deciduous plants that let warm rays through in winter and cast dappled shadows in summer.

If you plan your patio area so that it can be seen from the kitchen window, you will gain an immediate impression of extra space – an effect that can be further enhanced if it is possible to use the same flooring, such as terracotta or slate, or similarly coloured materials. Wide french windows or a glazed door will reduce the visual barrier between outside and inside and you can strengthen the garden link with botanical prints on the kitchen walls, a pretty floral blind, even a flowery apron.

Conservatories

An alternative – or an addition – to a patio, that will beat the most spiteful vagaries of the weather, is a conservatory. Long associated with gracious mansions, it is now finding itself at home even in modest gardens.

In order to reap year-round benefit, a conservatory should be sited to catch as much winter sun as possible. All windows and doors need to be thoroughly draughtproofed, and in cooler climates, double glazing or some sort of heating is almost essential. Don't, however, underestimate how hot a conservatory can be at the height of summer. There should be at least two large opening windows in the roof to allow the heat to escape.

Off-the-peg conservatories can be bought, or you can have one tailor-made to your own requirements. Make sure the design you choose doesn't have any inaccessible valleys that may get clogged with leaves. Toughened glass should be used for doors and windows; on the roof panels it should be laminated

Kettle The Bay Tree

to reduce the risk of breakage should a tile or slate slip from the roof of the house. Ideally, double glass doors should link the kitchen and the garden room. If the room will be used regularly as an eating area, remember that swing doors are easiest to operate when you are carrying a laden tray. Conservatories are not just for daytime: the design should also incorporate subtle lighting for night-time use.

Most conservatories need some sort of shading to screen out the fiercest summer sun. The choice ranges from simple roller blinds to sophisticated automatic devices. If you need blinds for privacy as well as shade, make sure they do the job and remain opaque when you have the lights on at night.

Fitting furniture

The type of furniture you choose will depend very much on the size of your patio or conservatory. If space is no object, you may prefer a table and chairs that are left permanently in place. For a patio, they should be heavy enough not to blow around and, even in a well sheltered spot, they must be fully weatherproof. This rules out wicker and cane although, if you like the romantic associations of wicker, you can look for traditional all-weather woven furniture, which is available at a price. Other options include cast iron, coated aluminium and the more sophisticated plastic furniture.

Even if the furniture can be left outside, it's advisable to bring the cushions in at the end of the day. Modern materials have improved greatly and the problems of mildew and rot are less likely to occur, but no technology, alas, can protect fabric from atmospheric dirt, bird droppings and non-colourfast leaves.

The classic choice for a conservatory is casual and comfortable: wicker and cane fit the bill perfectly here, but they tend to be bulky. If you want to use the room as a second dining room you need to choose compact pieces. Look at chairs and tables that are slightly lower than standard dining room furniture and take into account the amount of space needed to move a chair up to and away from the table – a minimum of one metre.

If space is limited, outdoors or indoors, look at lightweight folding furniture that can be brought out and put away easily as required.

A small patio leading off the kitchen provides a pleasant setting for a meal or entertaining guests

In order to reap year-round benefit, a conservatory should be sited to catch as much winter sun as possible.

Conservatories often become the most well-used room in the house

Alexander Bartholomew Conservatories Ltd

For both patios and conservatories, an old fashioned trolley can be a boon when it comes to serving and clearing away; the trolley may also be useful for storing condiments, place mats and the like.

For safety's sake, especially when children are around, it is worth investing in non-breakable plates and acrylic glasses for outdoor eating. There is a wonderful range of bright and sophisticated designs available.

A place for plants

Plants, of course, play a vital role in establishing a relaxed and pleasant atmosphere. Start with some evergreens, such as conifers and ivy outside, or ferns and palms in a conservatory. Ring seasonal changes with bulbs and colourful bedding plants. Make the most of the kitchen connection and grow your own decorative foods: herbs, tomatoes, chillies and peppers, even a grape vine, all will flourish in sheltered, sunny conditions. Citrus trees in tubs will also thrive as long as they are protected from frost; their flowers smell heavenly and you may even have a fruitful harvest.

TIPSTRIP

Drawings, paintings or photographs of vegetables or flowers look wonderful in the kitchen. They need not be expensive prints. A watercolour illustration or photograph of an artichoke, for example, can be cut out of a magazine and simply framed.

Project 9

Making a kitchen garden

Your kitchen garden can be as simple as a few herbs in pots outside your back door, or a proper vegetable and herb garden.

The type of garden you choose will depend upon the space you have available, the amount of sun it gets, the time you have to spend in the garden, and to a certain extent, your own taste in food. A small-scale kitchen garden could perhaps consist of a few herbs and some tomatoes, lettuce and carrots.

Siting the garden

You'll need a spot close to the kitchen which gets plenty of sun (at least two-thirds of the day) and is protected from strong winds. Border your site with bricks, stones or logs and dig in a good quality organic material such as compost or well-rotted manure. Special attention to soil condition at this stage will repay you handsomely later on.

The compost heap

Starting a compost heap is easy. Heap your lawn clippings, stray leaves and vegetable waste from the kitchen into a pile, keep it moist and regularly turned and when it has broken down scatter it over your garden to provide organic material which will replenish the soil.

Succession planting

The key to providing enough vegetables for your family over the whole growing season is succession planting. If you sow too many seeds at the one time you'll have a glut of vegetables and then nothing. Plant only six vegetables every fortnight, selecting varieties with different maturing dates. Seed

COMPANION PLANTING CHART	
Plant	**Compatible with**
beans	cauliflower, rosemary, sage
cabbages	beetroot, celery, onions, tomatoes, dill, mint, oregano, thyme, nasturtium
carrots	peas, lettuce, radish, chives
lettuce	carrots, strawberries, radishes, cabbage, beetroot
onions	beetroot, carrots, lettuce, cabbage
peas	radishes, carrots, cucumber, beans
tomatoes	basil, parsley, cabbage, marigolds, chives, carrots, borage, garlic, lemon balm, parsley

Avoid planting strawberries near the cabbage family and peas and beans with the onion family.

packets and labels will often indicate 'early', 'mid-season' or 'late'. This way you will have new plants coming on as the older ones mature.

Intercropping

This is particularly useful when space is a problem. The idea is to plant two vegetables close together – tall slender growers such as onions or leeks can be interspersed with compact growers such as lettuce and radish. Or lettuce and spinach can be grown with tomatoes – the leaf vegetables will mature before the tomatoes overshadow them. If you plant radishes close to carrots, the radishes will mature first and help to loosen the soil.

Crop rotation

The principle is that a crop of light feeding plants should follow a crop of heavy feeders.

A kitchen garden can be as simple as a few herbs in pots

Denise Greig

TIPSTRIP

Safe garden pesticides include those based on soaps and garlic. Or make your own by boiling rhubarb leaves in water for 20 minutes. Strain, cool and pour over your vegetables.

This maintains soil texture and fertility and controls pests and diseases at the same time. Leaf crops such as lettuce and spinach, which use plenty of nitrogen, should be followed by root crops such as carrots and radishes, which do not. Peas and beans return nitrogen to the soil and raise trace elements from lower layers which can be used by surface rooting vegetables. Do not plant members of the same family in the same spot in successive years.

Companion planting

This is planting one particular vegetable or herb with another for their mutual benefit. For example, basil planted close to tomatoes deters the white fly which transmits fungal diseases. Garlic keeps aphids and red spider mites away from tomatoes but should not be planted close to peas, beans, cabbages and strawberries. Marigolds prevent root-rotting bacteria and nasturtiums are a useful general insect repellent.

This kind of organic gardening gives many benefits:

❏ It prevents the soil degradation that comes from too-frequent use of chemical fertilisers.

❏ Beneficial soil organisms, such as worms and bacteria will thrive, aerating the soil and preventing diseases.

❏ Natural predators such as birds will rid the garden of pests. At the same time as helping the environment, you get fresh, healthy vegetables and herbs.

Heating and cooling

The perfect kitchen is toasty and warm in winter, cool and airy in summer but, alas, the situation is often reversed.

The floor

However magnificent they may look in an old farmhouse, cold, grey flagstone floors don't conjure up a sense of winter comfort. The fact is, if your feet are cold, so is the rest of you. Ironically, in the right location, solid floors are an important factor in maintaining a good ambient temperature.

The 'right location' is a room that enjoys sunshine for most of the day. Stone and other solid materials, like concrete and brick, absorb heat while the air temperature is high; this has the effect of cooling the room. When the air temperature drops, the laws of nature dictate that the heat is released again, and the room will be warmed. In summer and winter alike, the temperature should remain pleasant and constant.

Even in a not-so-sunny situation, you can capitalise on a solid floor's ability to store heat. Underfloor heating elements set into the concrete slab, can be installed at the time of building or renovating. Once the floor has warmed up, it gives out a constant, even temperature and it is quite economical to keep the heat 'topped up'. Because it is slow to respond, however, this type of heating is not suitable for, say, a weekend cottage. By the time it had warmed up you would be packing your bags and heading back to town.

Stone or ceramic tiles are good flooring choices unless you have a solid floor that does not get any sunshine and doesn't have heating beneath. Then some sort of insulation between the floor and your feet is essential. A rug is fine in the dining area but not advisable in the kitchen, where it may slip, or trip people up. Instead, think about laying cork tiles or cushioned vinyl sheeting. Most carpets are not suitable for kitchen use but there are tight-looped synthetic carpets which are very resistant to staining (but which will melt), and heavy duty carpet tiles which can be lifted for cleaning and, if necessary, be replaced.

Heating well

In a centrally heated house, it seems obvious to incorporate a radiator or hot air outlet in the kitchen – but in this era of fitted units it can be hard to find an appropriate spot. Radiators, fortunately, are available in a huge variety of shapes and sizes, from tall and thin to long and low. Hot air outlets should be kept as low as possible (hot air rises) and can sometimes be incorporated into the plinths of the units. In the interests of efficiency and economy, don't position a source of heat next to the fridge or freezer.

If you're using a plug-in appliance, make sure that the flex doesn't trail across the traffic area.

Kitchen comfort

The thought of a big, cosy stove is very comforting in inclement weather and the appeal of the Aga stove and similar models remains strong. Solid fuel models are still available, or you can opt for the convenience of gas or oil. Many people love cooking on these stoves and enjoy the other benefits: hot water and heating for the house. Disadvantages are that they generate heat in summer too, and the kitchen must be well ventilated to allow the excess warmth to disperse.

Keeping cool

The simplest form of ventilation is, of course, an open window but in summer it can let in more than fresh air. Simple mesh screens will keep flies, mosquitoes and moths at bay while letting cooking fumes escape and cooling breezes in to soothe the harassed cook.

Windows alone, however, can rarely cope with the heat and smells created by frying and grilling. If you do not have a rangehood (cooker hood), think about installing an extractor fan (see page 69). Because the fan will cut out light if installed in a window, it is preferable to mount it in an outside wall. The supplier should advise you on the best location – it should be close to the source of fumes but should not be positioned so that it creates a draught that 'drags' flames towards it.

The model you buy must be powerful enough for the size of your room and, ideally, should have several speeds. Other features to look for are timer switches, efficient draught proofing when the fan is not in use, air intake as well as expulsion and a strong outer grille.

Aga-Rayburn

A gas-fired Aga cooker can add character and warmth to a kitchen as well as deal with the practical aspects of cooking

At the heart of every efficient kitchen is a well-ordered storage system for food and utensils. To make the most of the space available, take time at the planning stage to think about your own requirements.

STORAGE SOLUTIONS

One of the most frequent laments about kitchens is that there is not enough storage space. Even apparently well-designed kitchens can have trouble accommodating the huge baking dish for the Christmas turkey, let alone empty bottles and piles of newspaper saved for recycling. More often than not, however, the problem is not so much the amount of space as the way in which it is used. Even in a large kitchen you need to plan carefully or you'll waste a lot of effort traipsing back and forth.

Well-organised storage should ease the work flow: foods should be stored close to the preparation equipment, which should be near the cooking equipment, which should be near the stove; crockery should be next to the dishwasher so that it's quick to put away; washing-up liquids and cleaning equipment are logically stored under the sink, because that's where they are most often to be used. It is really a matter of common sense rather than set rules. You're better off keeping the tea and teapot next to the kettle rather than storing them in different places.

Taking stock

If you are reorganising your kitchen storage, start by establishing exactly what is there. Have a fairly ruthless clear-out and get rid of anything that hasn't been used for years – if ever you suddenly needed it, the chances are that you wouldn't remember where it was. Infrequently used, but necessary, items that come out for highdays and holidays don't have to be kept in the kitchen – suitable alternatives include under the stairs, on top of the wardrobe, in the attic or in the garage.

Once you are down to essential, regularly used items, you can work out the best way to use the space available. The most frequently used items should be given the most easily reached space: that is, anywhere between eye level and knee level. Anything that is used less than once a week has no business gathering dust and cluttering up the worktop. Small items need special consideration, too. Be they birthday candles or butter curlers, they will be lost or forgotten if allowed to drift to the back of a deep cupboard or the bottom of a drawer.

The classic kitchen

work triangle allows for food storage and preparation, cooking, serving and washing up, and the storage zones should be arranged accordingly. To help you maximise every centimetre available, there are dozens of ideas and options available for the kitchen – from the simple and effective to the downright ingenious.

Out in the open

Storage doesn't have to be behind closed doors or hidden in drawers. A drawer full of kitchen utensils, for instance, is usually chaotic. Even if it is divided into compartments, things like whisks and fish slices never quite seem to fit.

One answer is to have all your favourite spoons and gadgets readily to hand. You can make your own wall storage with a piece of pegboard and some hooks, or you can buy one of the many sleek commercial variations on the theme. These include plastic coated or plain metal grids and polished steel rods that are designed to go between the worktop and the wall units. The latter will also take other accessories such as holders for kitchen rolls. A utensil jar next to

the stove keeps wooden spoons under control.

Magnetic racks or wooden blocks should be used for sharp knives, which should never be kept in a drawer, partly because the blades are likely to be blunted, more because you may cut

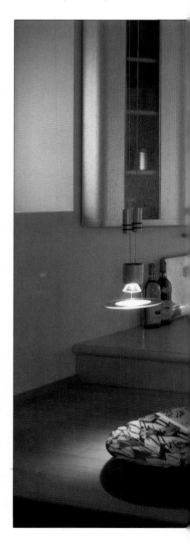

HTH Kitchens

Cabinetcraft Kitchens

Well-organised storage should ease the work flow: store foods near preparation equipment, which should be near the cooking equipment, which should be close to the stove.

yourself while searching for the knife you want. For true open-plan storage, suspend a rail from the ceiling and hang sauce-pans, sieves and colanders along its length. Don't underestimate the benefits of having food on show. Not all fresh produce has to be stored in the fridge. Many fruits – apples, pears, bananas, tomatoes – taste better at room temperature and look pretty, too. Dried herbs, garlic and eggs can also serve a decorative as well as a culinary purpose. Open shelves with jars and containers can look very

Kitchen Architecture

Cabinetcraft Kitchens

Cabinetcraft Kitchens

Left: Storage does not mean hiding everything. Kitchen utensils can look great when hung from the wall or gathered in a wooden holder
Above right: Plate shelves are an interesting solution to stacking plates in high cupboards
Right: A wine rack fits neatly underneath a workbench and makes maximum use of space

attractive, especially in a country-style kitchen. Although glass and clear plastic look good and display the contents, remember that some foods deteriorate in bright light. In a sunny room, opaque containers are better.

Easy access

Ideally, canned and dry food should be stored on shallow shelves so that you can see at a glance what's there. In practice, most people have to store provisions in a cupboard that is the same depth as the rest of the kitchen units – but this doesn't necessarily mean rummaging around in search of that elusive tin of soup.

A practical solution is to reduce the depth of fixed shelves and use the back of the doors to carry narrow shelves or racks. Another alternative is shelves that slide out or, indeed, an entire larder unit that rolls out. These enable you to see and reach right to the back of the unit. Sliding shelves are a boon for crockery storage as well, and put an end to reaching over a precarious pile of bowls to the plates beyond. Very shallow drawers are good for place mats; wide, deep drawers house bulky pans and baking dishes.

One of the tried and trusted means of reaching into awkward corners is the carousel unit. While it is true that they don't make use of every last centimetre of space, this is more than made up for by the increased accessibility. Many an electrical gadget languishes unused because it is too much trouble to take it out of storage.

An appliance cupboard with plenty of power outlets makes sure that toaster, coffee grinder, food processor and more are ready for action. When not in use, they are behind closed doors, not cluttering up the worktop.

Space stealers

In a well-planned kitchen there need be no such thing as wasted space. Even a gap a measly 18 cm wide can be put to work as a broom cupboard; shelves a mere 7.5 cm deep are perfect for storing and displaying canned foods or glasses. The space between the worktop and the wall cupboards is often wasted. Use it for keeping small things under control – spice jars, egg cups, pepper grinder. Many kitchen manufacturers now offer these midway units along with numerous other ingenious schemes for utilising otherwise lost space. At least one company has a two-tier cutlery drawer to hold more cutlery with less clutter. Kitchen steps that fold up and tuck into the kick plate, kick plate drawers that hold a tool kit, pull-out work surfaces and chopping boards are other nifty ideas. They tend to be pricey, but if space is at a premium in your kitchen they can be a godsend.

HTH Kitchens

Goldreif – Kitchen Architecture

*Left: An extra work surface is incorporated into a drawer
Below left: These shelves pull out from the wall and, when closed, follow the line of the kitchen
Right: The modern look of this kitchen is achieved by fitting the appliances into the walls so they are in line with the cupboards. Storage space is all within easy reach and shelving space is well utilised*

Juicer and Bowl Paraphernalia

Below: A midway storage rack and hooks allows utensils and other implements to be kept close at hand

In a well-planned kitchen there need be no such thing as wasted space. Even a gap a measly 18 cm wide can be put to work as a broom cupboard; shelves a mere 7.5 cm deep are perfect for storing and displaying canned foods or glasses.

HTH Kitchens

Project 10

Shelves and storage

In any kitchen, but especially a small kitchen, where space is at a premium, it is important to make use of all available space for storage.

These DIY projects will enable you to keep kitchen essentials within easy reach. While they are simple to make, they look smart and help keep your kitchen neat.

All these projects are suitable for novice carpenters.

Saucepan lid drawer

Saucepan lids are awkward to store but if you make this practical rack to fit a deep drawer, you will always be able to find the right lid to fit every saucepan when you need it.

STEP BY STEP

1 Cut spacers to a height of 15 mm less than the depth of the drawer (measuring from the inside).

2 Cut spacers to length (see detail A).

3 Glue and nail these spacers to the inside of your drawer sides allowing 7 mm between them (make sure the nails do not protrude through the drawer sides).

4 Cut dividers to width and length and slip into place.

MATERIALS	TIME
6 mm plywood PVA adhesive nails	2 hours
TOOLS	
saw tape measure ruler hammer	

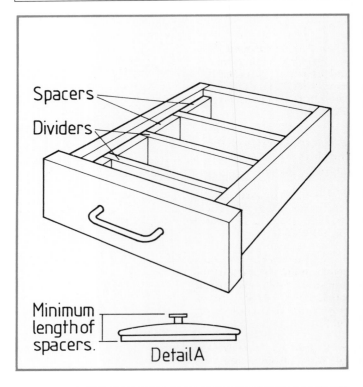

Spacers
Dividers
Minimum length of spacers.
Detail A

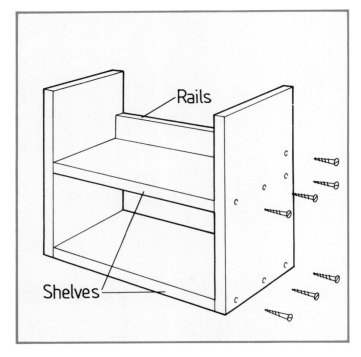

Rails
Shelves

Bookshelves

The size of these shelves will vary depending upon the space available and the number of books you want to display.

STEP BY STEP

1 Cut shelves and rail to the same length.

2 Cut ends to size and drill holes for screws.

3 Screw and glue the unit together. Drill for the screws and countersink the holes with a countersinking bit in your drill.

4 Sand and paint or lacquer in your choice of colour.

MATERIALS	
Suggested timber sizes: **ends and shelves** 200 x 25 mm **rail** 50 x 25 mm (these are nominal sizes; planed sizes are slightly smaller) screws 50 mm x 8 gauge PVA adhesive	
TOOLS	**TIME**
mitre box or similar saw screwdriver or power driver sanding block and paper	3 hours

Plate rack

This simple folding plate rack is elegant and convenient as well as relatively easy to make. The material is all stock size so it is readily available at your timber yard

STEP BY STEP

1 Cut 27 legs from 25 x 25 mm DAR (PAR) softwood to 350 mm long.

2 Drill a 4 mm diameter hole for the bolt 125 mm from one end of each leg. A vertical drill stand is best but it can be done carefully by hand with an electric drill.

3 Insert the bolt into the holes and fit the nuts and washers but do not tighten.

4 Insert cardboard spacers (approximately 1 mm thick) between legs and finger-tighten the bolt (see fig. 1).

5 Lay the assembly flat on a bench and screw and glue the top rail on at 100 mm below the top of the legs. Make sure you only screw to alternate legs (see fig. 2).

6 Repeat step 5 for bottom rail, 97 mm from bottom.

7 Turn the assembly over and repeat steps 5 and 6 but ensure that you are screwing the rails to the opposite legs (i.e. legs without screws on the other side).

8 Cut rails to length where they overhang and sand flush.

9 Remove cardboard spacers and sand and paint in your choice of colour.

The wooden plate rack can be positioned on the sink or just next to it for handy access when washing dishes

MATERIALS	TOOLS
legs 27 lengths of 25 x 25 mm DAR (PAR) softwood at 350 mm long	tape measure
rails 4 lengths of 25 x 25 mm DAR (PAR) softwood, approx 500 mm long	drill
screws 54 of 32 mm x 8 gauge, countersunk	saw
bolt 4 x 520 mm, brass, chrome or galvanised steel threaded full length with 2 nuts and washers to suit	screwdriver
waterproof adhesive	sanding block
lacquer or paint	countersinking bit

TIME

3½ hours

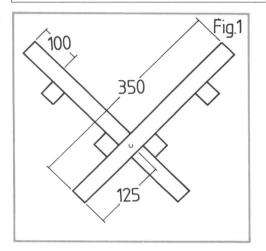

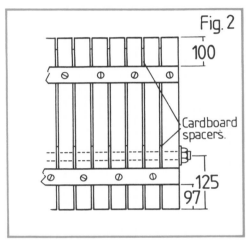

Left: The wooden wine rack is simple to make and will hold a large number of bottles

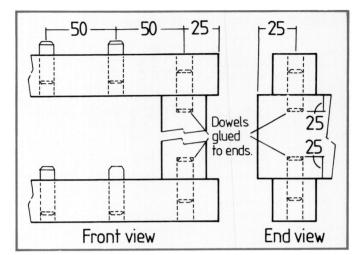

Front view   End view

Dowels glued to ends.

Wine rack

Here is a simple wine rack that you should be able to make in 4 hours.

All the timber is stock size so it will be readily available from your local timber supplier.

STEP BY STEP

1 Cut the ends to 270 mm long and drill 8 mm holes in both edges at both ends, four holes in all. The holes are in the centre of the edges, 25 mm deep and 25 mm from ends.

2 Cut the rails to length (700 mm) and drill 8 mm holes 50 mm apart, starting 25 mm from the ends. Drill all holes right through the rails.

3 Glue the dowels into the rails in all holes with the exception of the end holes. Make sure that the dowels finish flush on the bottom.

4 Glue four dowels into the ends and make sure that they are hammered right down.

5. Sand and paint or varnish as required and assemble.

MATERIALS	
6 lengths of 100 x 38 mm DAR (PAR) softwood at 270 mm 8 lengths of 38 x 38 mm DAR (PAR) softwood at 700 mm 120 38 x 8 mm furniture dowels PVA adhesive paint or varnish sandpaper	

TOOLS	TIME
saw 8 mm drill bit drill hammer	4 hours

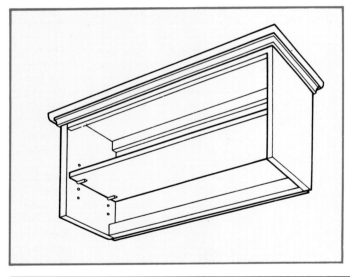

Dresser shelves

This simple dresser can be made to any size, although if it is to be wider than a metre the shelves may begin to sag if a lot of heavy china is placed on it.

It is designed to sit on top of a worktop or sideboard. Screw the unit to the wall to stop it falling forward.

STEP BY STEP

1 Cut the wood for the ends to length and drill for adjustable shelf supports.

2 Cut front and back rails to length (three in all, one at the front top and two at the back).

3 Screw and glue rails between ends and glue and nail plywood to the back to hold it square.

4 Cut top 40 mm wider and 80 mm longer than size of unit and round ends and front with a plane and sandpaper or an electric router.

5 Cut and fit scotia moulding under top glue and nail. Use a mitre box to achieve 45° cuts.

6 Cut shelves to length (1 mm clearance each end).

7 Glue and nail a thin strip of wood as a plate stop to front edge of shelves if required. Paint or lacquer in the colour of your choice. If painting be sure to undercoat properly first.

8 Insert shelf supports and install shelves. Shelf supports may be proprietary metal rods, cut lengths of aluminium rod (3-4 mm) or dowel.

MATERIALS	TOOLS	
top 200 x 25 mm DAR (PAR) softwood **ends and shelves** 150 x 25 mm DAR (PAR) softwood **rails** 38 x 25 mm softwood **back** 6 mm ply **moulding** 25 mm scotia paint or varnish	saw ruler square screwdriver	mitre box hammer drill
	TIME	
	4-6 hours	

Rubbish and fume disposal

Every day in every kitchen, an enormous amount of waste is generated.

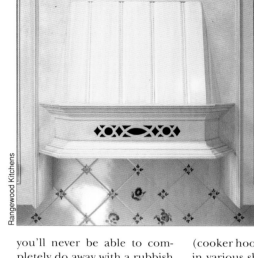

This extractor fan is cleverly hidden in an interesting wooden hood with carved details

Rangewood Kitchens

Waste comes in all shapes and forms – paper, cardboard, plastic, food scraps, liquids, oils, even airborne waste – the list goes on, and we all create literally mountains of the stuff.

A lot of our rubbish is a product of modern packaging methods, particularly in the case of cardboard wrapping, plastic bags and containers and metal cans. We can all do our bit by refusing to buy over-packaged products. It's easy enough to cut down on plastic carrier bags by recycling them or by using canvas or string bags.

However, that still leaves a lot of waste to deal with, and there are alternatives to just throwing it in the bin.

If you have a spare corner of the garden that's dry and well drained, think about making a compost heap. This is an ideal way of getting rid of all sorts of organic waste – food scraps, egg shells, coffee grounds and tea leaves, as well as wood shavings, newspaper, grass clippings, leaves and natural fibre clothes. Add fresh waste regularly, rather than occasional large deposits. Every 30 cm or so, add a layer of soil or manure, and, to prevent the top layer drying out, cover with an old damp sack.

For other types of rubbish, find out if there are council pick-ups for recyclable material such as paper, glass, plastic or aluminium; or alternatively there may be a deposit centre in your area.

Even if you do manage to get rid of most of your rubbish in an ecologically sound way, you'll never be able to completely do away with a rubbish bin somewhere in your kitchen. You can choose from the traditional freestanding bin, or, especially if you are designing a new kitchen, plan to have a concealed one, usually in a cupboard under the sink.

Another possibility for getting rid of kitchen waste is to have a waste disposer fitted to the sink. Electrically operated, it is attached under the sink waste outlet and grinds rubbish into fine particles. These are then washed down the drain and become part of the already overburdened sewerage system. In a high rise flat, a waste disposer may be acceptable, but for anyone with a garden, the food scraps that are eaten up by the unit would be put to far better use on the compost heap.

Airborne smells in kitchens – the dreaded boiled cabbage or grilled chops – can permeate the whole house if they are not dealt with close to the source when they're produced. Water vapour from cooking can cause condensation problems in the room, leading to mould spots and rotting window frames. Opening a window or the back door is the obvious answer, but that's not always possible or practical.

The most effective way of getting rid of smells and water vapour is to install a rangehood (cooker hood). These come in various shapes and sizes, either off-the-shelf or custom-made. They can be completely inconspicuous; either installed behind a hinged door which, when opened, activates the mechanism, or the telescopic variety, a slimline unit which, when not in use, can be pushed back in to sit flush with adjacent cupboards. Otherwise, a feature can be made of the hood; in beaten copper for the country kitchen, or stainless steel for a more modern look.

You can also find extractors fitted into the worktop as part of the cooking hob itself. Installed below the worktop, the only part you see is a metal grille. This type of extractor is much more expensive than the more conventional type.

One word of advice before buying an extractor – try it out in the showroom first by holding a piece of paper to it. If the paper attaches itself, the extractor will probably be powerful enough for your needs. If it doesn't, keep looking, or open a window.

A canopy rangehood fits neatly over a kitchen island and is positioned above the cooktop (hob)

Omega-Smeg

Refrigerators and freezers

Fridges and freezers are no longer huge white shapes looming in the corner. While they may be less bulky on the outside, their internal capacity is what counts for most people.

Despite all the streamlining, size, more than any other factor, determines which model of fridge or freezer we buy. A tall larder fridge and a matching freezer give ample easily accessible storage space but many kitchens are simply not big enough to accommodate them. Alternatives include a freezer kept separately – in the utility room, garage or wherever – or a combined fridge/freezer unit. Whatever you buy, choose a model on which the door is hinged correctly – it should not open into the central space of the kitchen.

Cold comforts

If the outer dimensions of the refrigerator are limited, the interior space should be as flexible as possible. Make sure all features really will be useful. Adjustable shelves and a facility for storing tall opened bottles are essential; egg racks are not and take up valuable space. If you use a lot of fresh vegetables, look for a good-sized crisper drawer; a butter compartment is handy – but not if you are on a cholesterol-free diet! Gadgets like drink dispensers and ice makers come into their own during hot weather – and kids love them all year round. A freezer compartment is not necessary if there is also a freezer in the room; if not, it

is useful for storing ice cubes and soon-to-be-eaten foods.

Icy conditions

Freezers come in chest or cupboard (upright) types. The former tends to hold more, but if you are not very organised, food at the bottom can be forgotten. The cupboard type has accessible drawers which conveniently divide the food into, say, meat, vegetables, desserts, bread and pastries.

Winning combinations

The advantage of a combined fridge/freezer is that it uses only as much floor space as one unit. Most people find a 50:50 or 60:40 fridge/freezer ratio the best, with the freezer section at the bottom. Combined appliances usually have only one compressor. This makes them quieter but, if there is a problem with the compressor, both sections are out of use.

Getting the best from your freezer

❑ A full freezer is more economical to run than a half full one. If food stocks are low, fill the drawers with loaves of bread or even newspaper.
❑ Put the freezer in a cool, dry place, not in a sunny spot or next to any other source of heat.
❑ Before freezing food, set the thermostat to its lowest.
❑ Wrap foods thoroughly to exclude all air and moisture.

❑ Don't put hot food into the freezer – it will cause condensation. Cool foods as quickly as possible by standing dishes in a bowl of cold water.
❑ Label foods clearly – lamb stew and chocolate mousse look alike when frozen.

Power failure

❑ Food will remain in good condition for at least 8 hours – provided you do not open the door to check it out.
❑ Stick the telephone number of the service engineer to the side of the freezer.
❑ Take out insurance against loss of freezer contents.
❑ If the freezer is not in the kitchen, invest in a freezer alarm to alert you to an excessive increase in temperature.

Defrosting the freezer

❑ Try to do this when stocks are low.
❑ Switch off the freezer and take out all the food. Wrap the food in thick newspaper and put it in the fridge if there is room, in a picnic cool box or even wrap it in a quilt.
❑ Let the ice melt naturally – scraping it off with sharp tools may damage the lining.
❑ Wipe the inside with warm

water and bicarbonate of soda.
❑ Switch the freezer to its lowest setting and wait at least an hour before replacing the food.

Getting the best from your fridge

❑ Don't overfill the fridge.
❑ Don't open the door more often than you have to, or leave it open for more than a few seconds.
❑ Cover all food to stop strong flavours from tainting other foods.
❑ The door is the weakest part of most fridges: don't overload it or force large items into narrow shelves.
❑ Cool hot food before putting it in the fridge.

Philips Whirlpool

Omega-Smeg

Stoves and cooktops

With such an enormous variety of stoves, ovens and cooktops (hobs) on the market it is essential to do a little homework before you buy.

Start by making a list of basic requirements. How much can you spend – and does that amount include installation? What fuel do you prefer – gas, electricity, solid fuel, oil? How much space do you have? Do you cook mainly for just one or two, with occasional dinner parties? Regularly entertain on a grand scale? Produce non-stop meals for the family and assorted friends? What sort of cooking do you do – baking, frying, grilling and barbecuing, steaming and stir-frying?

Armed with this information you can identify the appliances that best suit you. If you do a lot of baking, look at a double oven; if you cook mainly 'on top', put the emphasis on a good-sized cooktop.

Which fuel?

Most cooks have a decided preference for one sort of fuel over another. Electricity is clean, convenient, readily available and much has been done by manufacturers to improve its performance. Electric ovens give an even heat throughout, so the food on the bottom rack cooks at the same rate as food at the top – ideal for batch baking.

Gas is highly controllable, quick to respond and, generally, cheaper than electricity. Gas ovens give 'zoned' temperatures, which is good if you are baking different foods at the same time. If you are a gas-lover living far from the nearest supply, consider an appliance that runs on LPG (keep a spare cylinder to hand).

Omega-Smeg

Kitchen ranges that run on gas, solid fuel or oil are wonderful in a traditional farmhouse kitchen and can perform various other functions too, such as heating the water or, indeed, the whole house. You don't have to stick to one fuel: many cooks find perfection with a quick responding gas cooktop and a clean electric oven.

Which type?

The appliances themselves fall into three main categories: free standing, built-in and slip-in.

While the traditional free-standing stove doesn't generally compete in the glamour stakes, it has its advantages. It is economical to buy and install; a drawer for storage or plate warming is very useful; there is usually a good-sized separate grill. To minimise cleaning problems, butt adjacent units right up to the stove and seal the gaps. If this is not possible, buy a model that has wheels or runners so that you can pull it out easily for cleaning.

Slip-in stoves are designed to fit flush with the units, giving a built-in appearance, but unlike built-ins they can be taken with you when you move house. The advantage of a built-in oven is that it can be installed at any convenient height and, because it is away from the cooktop, heat from the oven doesn't add to the discomfort of the cook. When buying a new oven check that the open door doesn't obstruct access to the dishes inside – particularly important in a wall oven. Controls should be positioned where they cannot be accidentally knocked. A glass door and an internal light show the progress of the food inside. In gas ovens, look for automatic ignition and a safety device that shuts off the gas should the flame extinguish.

Cooktops

Cooktops are available for electricity, gas and bottled gas. The most popular format remains the four rings arranged in a square, but variations include elongated elements for fish kettles and deep fryers. On gas cooktops, pan supports have always tended, for some reason, to be dirt-traps. The problem hasn't been totally overcome, but some designs are more streamlined than others. Totally flush ceramic and glass cooktops, on the other hand, come clean with a wipe, if you are diligent about clearing up spills as they occur. If allowed to burn on you may need to scrape them off gently with a sharp razor blade: no abrasive cleaners should be used on these cooktops.

Responsiveness has also improved. While the solid hotplate still has its fans, the new breed of cooktops uses halogen heat and magnetic induction, both of which offer precise control. Halogen cooktops glow when warm and magnetic induction tops don't get hot; on other cooktops a warning light that comes on when an element is in use and remains on until it has cooled is an invaluable safety device. On any electric cooktop it is important to use flat-bottomed pans for maximum contact with the heat source. Make sure that pan bases and cooktop are dry before use or the steam created will make the pans dance.

Above left: A stainless steel hob and oven
Below: Halogen and fast-start ceramic hobs are electrically powered and allow infinite heating adjustment

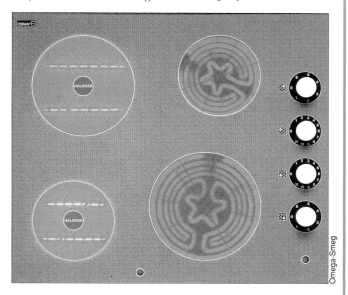
Omega-Smeg

Microwave ovens

The new generation of microwave ovens sports an impressive array of sophisticated options, but think carefully before you spend money on features you may not use.

Bosch

Owners of microwave ovens seem to fall into two categories: those who genuinely use them as an alternative means of cooking, and those who use them for defrosting and reheating – and until you have tried one, it is hard to know whether a basic model will suit you or whether you would get real benefit from the extra features offered by the more expensive models.

Making waves

All microwave ovens work on the same principle. Microwaves – very short high frequency radio waves – pass through the food and make the moisture molecules vibrate rapidly; this creates the heat that cooks the food. The microwaves bounce around randomly in the oven and, to ensure even cooking, some sort of distribution device is required: wave stirrers (fans), a turntable or both. Debate continues as to which is the more efficient.

A turntable limits the shape of dish you use (large square ones are likely to catch on the walls of the oven) and makes it impractical to include a shelf.

Every oven includes a timer and power settings ranging from about 90W to 650W or 700W. Simpler models may have several preset levels, while top-of-the-range ovens offer fully variable settings and additional features. Whether or not you buy an oven sporting all these aids is down to personal preference; the size, however, is an essential factor. If you prepare a lot of meals for one person, a small-capacity oven will suit your needs. If you cook for a crowd you must have a larger one – even if only to defrost a family-size pizza!

If your oven is not built in, be prepared to lose a lot of bench space or install a special shelf at a convenient height.

Combined forces

A single oven which can be used for both conventional and microwave cooking is an attractive prospect. It reduces the amount of space taken up by your cooking equipment, and it overcomes the chief disadvantage of microwave cooking: that foods do not brown. You can use either method on its own or alternate bursts of both.

Project 11

Microwave shelf

This shelf can be made to any length to suit your requirements.

Your microwave will have vents on the end or top which require at least 50 mm of clear space opposite them.

STEP BY STEP

1 Securely fix the steel brackets to the wall. The brackets should be buttressed, of galvanised or plastic-coated steel and large

enough to support the microwave without actually using a shelf. Use good quality masonry bolts if your wall is brick, or screw directly into the studs if it is a timber-frame wall. Do not hang brackets on cavity fixings such as toggle bolts.

2 Cut shelf to length. Use two or three widths of softwood as

required; they will be held together by the screws from the L-bracket. Sand and/or chamfer the ends.

3 Cut end to size and screw and glue it to the shelf once it is installed.

4 Paint or lacquer the shelf as required.

MATERIALS		
softwood, 20 x 20 mm thick, width as required		
shelf brackets minimum size 300 x 300 x 18 x 6 mm		
PVA adhesive	heavy-duty wall plugs	
screws	paint or lacquer	

TOOLS		TIME
hammer	handsaw	2 hours
hammer drill	sanding block	
screwdriver	paintbrush	

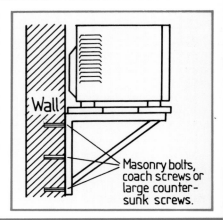

Wall

Masonry bolts, coach screws or large countersunk screws.

Dishwashers

Dishwashers are no longer considered luxury appliances. They are near-necessities in the modern kitchen.

If you still feel traces of guilt about using a dishwasher, take heart: it is a much more hygienic method of washing up – tea towels and dish cloths are perfect breeding grounds for germs – and, if you choose the model with care, it uses no more power and water than washing up by hand.

A few checks will make sure you are happy with the model you buy. First, find out the length of the shortest and the longest cycles, and the amount of water used – the lower the numbers, the kinder it is to your pocket and the environment. Does the machine have to be plumbed to the cold water supply? If you have abundant gas-heated hot water, it seems silly to pay for the machine to heat water from cold electrically. Some machines can be plumbed into the hot water system, a few models are both hot and cold fill. If you have a kitchen that is too small for a plumbed-in machine, there are worktop models and machines which can be stored elsewhere and then connected to the kitchen tap.

Capacity

Dishwashers with no central column are the most spacious. Most standard 600 mm models will hold 12 or 14 international place settings – that is, soup, dinner and dessert plate, glass, cup and saucer, soup spoon, knife, fork, dessertspoon and teaspoon – plus serving dishes.

If your service has oval plates or unusually large dishes, or you have very long-stemmed glasses, there may be problems fitting them in. Look for adjustable baskets and racks – on some models the upper rack can be lowered to accommodate tall glasses. Sliding racks facilitate loading and unloading; a removable bottom rack makes it easier to reach and remove the filter for cleaning.

Taking control

Washing programs are selected by dials, push buttons or touch controls. Some machines indicate what stage of the cycle has been reached; others have helpful warnings when water softeners or rinse aids are running low. Some sort of childproofing is a worthwhile feature if there are likely to be toddlers about.

The number of programs varies. While the idea of having several options is appealing, in practice most people end up using only one or two on a regular basis. Short economy cycles are invaluable for lightly soiled crockery or if you need dishes quickly – at a dinner party, entree dishes can be washed during the main course and re-emerge as dessert plates.

Another feature worth looking out for is a drying cycle that can be turned off: most dishes will dry in residual heat, albeit more slowly.

A noise annoys

A dishwasher that sounds like a jumbo jet taking off and can only be used when the family's gone to bed or left the house is hardly a modern convenience. Unfortunately, the noise level is one of the hardest aspects to check – although manufacturers of quiet machines are very keen to tell you about it – and all machines will grow noisier as they get old and worn. Machines that are built into a run of units, with insulation around them, tend to be quieter than free-standing models.

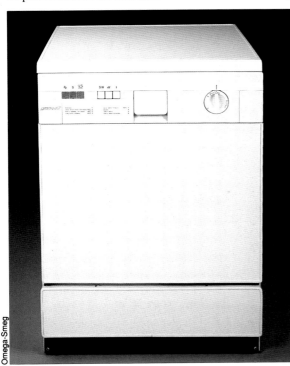
Omega-Smeg

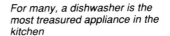
For many, a dishwasher is the most treasured appliance in the kitchen

Tips for top performance

❏ Follow the manufacturers' instructions regarding the type of detergent to use. Preferably, use the same brand of detergent and rinse aid.

❏ Don't use too much detergent – excess suds will stop the machine from operating efficiently and can leave a chalky film on china and glass.

❏ If a film still starts to appear, check the level of the rinse aid and try a different brand of detergent.

❏ Follow instructions about loading: dishes should face the spray and large items shouldn't shield smaller ones.

❏ Glass, plastic and wooden handled cutlery should be washed at a low temperature.

❏ Cups, bowls and glasses should have their rims tilted downwards so that they don't fill with water.

❏ Don't wash stainless steel and silver together – the silver can be stained and pitted. All cutlery should be removed as soon as possible when the cycle is complete.

❏ Don't put plastic items near the heating element as they may distort or melt.

❏ Secure plastic and lightweight items (like lids) with other dishes so they don't fall and block the filter or jam the runners.

❏ Make sure large items like baking trays don't hamper the action of the jets – the arms should be able to rotate freely.

❏ Do not wash thin plastic, valuable glassware or china, antique or hand-painted china, china decorated with silver or gold (it will gradually wear off), crystal (it will turn opaque), lacquered metal, pewter, iron, or wooden dishes.

Kids in the kitchen

Not for nothing is the kitchen called the heart of the home.

The family tends to gravitate towards the kitchen at all times of the day and, while it must serve primarily as a food preparation area, it's good if it also has a comfortable, companionable and welcoming atmosphere.

If there are children in the house, try to incorporate a space in the kitchen where they can play, paint and draw and, when they're older, do their homework. It will allow you to keep an eye on them while you get on with your own tasks and, at the same time, provide them with occupation, education and company.

From the earliest age, children are intrigued by the kitchen. It is, after all, the place where parents spend a lot of time, it's the source of food and, above all, it's filled with grown-ups' toys. These 'toys' can spell danger to un-supervised youngsters (see Safety below) but it is possible to organise the kitchen so that it gives pleasure to both parent and child.

At the crawling stage, a playpen keeps the baby out of harm's way and reduces the chances of your tripping over scattered toys. Make sure you can see each other and, so that he doesn't feel left out, give the child some safe kitchen utensils to play with. A spoon and a plastic jelly mould or, if you can stand the noise, a saucepan will do nicely as musical instruments. A child who can stand and walk is going to want a more active involvement – washing up and cooking are still fun at this age. Invest in sturdy steps so that she can reach the sink and worktop; a pinafore-type apron that offers maximum protection to clothes is also a good idea. A sinkful of sudsy water and some plastic beakers, or a bowl of flour and water 'dough' will keep pre-schoolers entertained for some time. Try to set up the play area away from where you are working so that you can get on with things unhindered and without having to watch for inquisitive fingers near the food processor. Resign yourself to the fact that the trade-off for this lack of interruption is that you will have to clear up puddles of water and spills of flour.

Older children will get pleasure, not just from playing with dough, but from making something, too. Simple biscuit recipes or jam tarts are good starting points, even if dolly, teddy and the dog eat most of the end products. As the child grows older, get him more involved with meal preparation. A simple explanation of why you are serving certain foods together will help lay the basis of good dietary knowledge.

Take advantage of a willingness to wash lettuce leaves and lay the table while it lasts. For some time this 'help' will undoubtedly slow things down rather than speed them up, so for the sake of your nerves, make allowances for this. After all, it's probably better to take an hour and have a happy child than half an hour and have a child who feels neglected.

Introducing children to the kitchen and aspects of safety and diet at an early age will help them understand the intrigue of the many 'toys' it contains

From the earliest age, children are intrigued by the kitchen. It is, after all, the place where parents spend a lot of time, it's the source of food and it's filled with grown-ups' toys. These 'toys' can spell danger to unsupervised youngsters.

Gradually introduce the child to the supervised use of kitchen tools and appliances. Moving blades, control knobs, glowing elements, flames and steam are all fascinating to a child and there is less risk of accidents if she understands how to use them. You may reap the benefits in other ways – with tea and toast brought to you in bed on Sunday morning.

SAFETY WITH CHILDREN IN MIND

❑ Keep appliance cords as short as possible (look for models that have cord storage): toddlers may well be tempted to yank on trailing cords.

❑ Cover all electric outlets that are not in use to stop inquisitive young fingers. Use purchased socket covers.

❑ Store knives and other sharp implements out of reach of children. Wall-mounted magnetic racks can be positioned safely; wooden knife blocks can be kept at the back of the work surface. Use plastic guards with food processor blades and electric knife blades.

❑ Be aware of possible risk items: serrated edges for cutting foil and film can cut young skin too; plastic film can cause suffocation.

❑ Whenever possible, cook on the back burners of the stove. Keep handles turned towards the back so that they cannot be knocked by passers-by or grabbed by children.

❑ Buy a stove guard to stop pans being pulled off the top of the stove.

❑ Make sure children are out of the way when you serve up hot food.

❑ Keep all household detergents, cleaners, bleaches, scourers and anything else that may possibly be poisonous on the highest shelf possible. Do not transfer the contents to soft drink bottles.

❑ Don't add dishwasher detergent until you are ready to switch on the machine.

❑ Fit childproof catches to all drawers and cupboards that contain anything that is potentially harmful. Remove those catches before disposing of cupboards, fridges and freezers – children, finding a new 'play house' have been known to get trapped.

❑ Keep all rubbish out of reach of children.

❑ Never leave an iron on when you leave the room, and don't let young children anywhere near the board while you are ironing.

The kitchen office

It's a good idea to set aside a corner of the kitchen as an office area. It doesn't have to be big – just a metre or so of bench space with room to tuck your knees under.

The first essential is, of course, a telephone. There are few things more infuriating – and potentially dangerous – than having to leave the room to answer the phone while you're cooking.

In addition you need shelves for cookery books and telephone directories, and a filing system for the inevitable accumulation of bills, receipts, guarantees and instruction booklets.

Information that you use regularly, such as rubbish collection days, baby sitters' telephone numbers, needs to be readily available: a notice board is simple and convenient, and is also handy for invitations, reminders and outstanding bills – not to mention junior's latest artistic offering. Keep a blackboard in a prominent place for family members to jot down shopping requirements as they notice supplies running low; the board also serves as a general message board ('Mum, please ring Gran'). A calendar with space to write on or, better still, a large year planner like the ones used in offices, is another essential. It enables you to see at a glance the school holiday dates; birthdays and anniversaries; medical check-up dates and other forgettable facts.

Organise infrequently used information in a house book. Divide an ordinary exercise book into sections for each room in the house, the exterior and the garden and record everything relevant to that area – all new purchases, the colour and brand of paint and the application date, telephone numbers of tradesmen. Such details are invaluable if two years later, say, you need to patch the flooring. Tracking down a replacement piece will be much easier if you can quote the manufacturer, exact style and colour.

Safety in the kitchen

Most accidents occur in the home and most home accidents occur in the kitchen.

By definition, the kitchen is one of the most dangerous rooms in the house – sharp edges and hot substances are an integral part of food preparation – but most accidents can be prevented. Here are some simple measures to make your kitchen a safer place.

❏ Choose non-slip flooring; always mop up spills immediately.

❏ Don't have scatter rugs in the main traffic area – they are too easy to trip over.

❏ Rounded corners on tables and worktops are less painful to bump into than square ones.

❏ Don't plug too many appliances into one outlet. Apart from the risk of overloading the supply, a tangle of cords is asking for trouble.

❏ Always switch off before unplugging an appliance.

❏ Use proper oven gloves, not teatowels, for removing dishes from the oven – ones that cover the wrists are best.

❏ Use sturdy kitchen steps to reach high cupboards. Don't carry out balancing acts on stools and worktops.

❏ Loose fabrics – curtains, flowing sleeves, trailing tea cloths – near the stove are a fire hazard.

❏ Know what to do if there is a fire (fat fires, for example, should be smothered; dousing them with water will make them worse). It's a good idea to keep a small fire extinguisher, suitable for fat and electric fires, or fire blanket next to the stove but make sure all family members understand exactly how to use them.

❏ If you suspect a gas leak, extinguish all naked flames. DON'T switch on anything electric – not even the lights – as a spark could ignite the gas, causing a major disaster.

❏ Discourage pets in the kitchen. On the floor, they're liable to trip you up; on tables and benches, they deposit dirt and hair.

Cleaning the kitchen

Supermarket shelves are filled with household cleaners, many of which are over-packaged and over-priced.

They contain not only promises of what they can do to make our lives easier, but also, quite often, very strong chemicals which can harm the environment and pose health hazards. There are alternatives – here are some tips that will save you money and help save the environment. Many of the products are ones you will already have on your shelves.

Bicarbonate of soda

❑ Rub stains in the sink with bicarb.

❑ Sprinkle bicarb on the walls and floor of a warm oven, leave for an hour, and then wipe clean.

❑ Dissolve bicarb in boiling water, and use to unblock drains.

❑ Clean glass doors with a damp cloth dipped in dry bicarb.

❑ To remove coffee and tea stains on cups, rub with a damp cloth dipped in dry bicarb.

❑ An open packet of bicarb left in the refrigerator after cleaning will deodorise it.

❑ Pour hot water on grease stains and cover with dry bicarb.

❑ Make a light paste of bicarb and water, and use as a mild abrasive to clean sinks, tiles and laminates.

❑ Add cold water and one or two teaspoons of bicarb to dirty saucepans, and bring to the boil. When cool, clean off with steel wool.

Vinegar

❑ Soak a paper towel in vinegar and leave it on hard-water deposits on the tap.

❑ Vinegar can sometimes be used to remove stains from marble – be careful, though, and try it in an inconspicuous spot to ensure that it does not affect the marble.

❑ Add a tablespoon of vinegar to washing-up water to help remove grease.

❑ Add one and a half cups of vinegar to one litre of water for cleaning windows.

❑ Use equal parts of vinegar and boiling water to defur the kettle.

❑ Use vinegar with soap to clean vinyl floors.

❑ Rub vinegar onto the stain that forms when a tap drips.

❑ To clean glassware, swill tea leaves and vinegar around the glass.

Lemon juice

❑ To clean inside a microwave, stand a dish of hot water with a slice of lemon in the oven. Boil the water until there is plenty of steam, and then wipe inside with a damp cloth.

❑ Corrosion spots on copper pans can be treated with lemon juice and salt. Leave for a while, then rinse and dry.

A well-planned kitchen with plenty of storage space is the easiest to keep clean

Tiffany Kitchens – Kitchen Architecture

❑ Rub dirty wall tiles with a cut lemon. Leave for about 15 minutes, then polish with a soft cloth.

❑ For rust stains, saturate with lemon juice and rub with salt. Place in sunlight until dry, then wash.

Salt, vinegar and bicarbonate of soda will clean your kitchen as effectively as many chemical products and help save the environment too. They're also kinder to your hands and much cheaper.

❑ Leave lemon juice overnight on stains on laminate and porcelain.

Pure soap

❑ Use a cake of pure soap in a wire basket for washing dishes.

❑ Use soap with a plastic scourer for cleaning laminates, tiles and stainless steel.

Washing soda

❑ Use as a water softener.

❑ Clean pots and pans by boiling with washing soda.

❑ Use with hot water to unblock drains.

❑ For heavy stains, rub a solution of 30 g washing soda in 250 mL warm water.

Salt

❑ Mix equal parts salt, vinegar and flour to make copper polish. Rub copper until clean, then rinse off in hot water and dry.

❑ Salt, mixed with lemon juice, removes rust stains.

Glossary

Architrave: The trim around the windows and doors.

Batten: Thin timber member supporting sheets, coverings or tiles.

Coach screws: Large screws with a hexagonal head, requiring a spanner to turn into place.

Course: A row (of bricks).

Crosshead screwdriver: Also called Phillips head, it is a screwdriver with a cross-shaped point.

Dado: The lower part of the wall, often to chair height, which may be defined by a moulding or border.

DAR (PAR): Dressed all round (Planed all round). Timber that is smooth, as in planed.

Dowel: Round timber.

Fixtures: Refers to lights, switch plates and other permanent items attached to walls.

Grout: The (compressible) filler between tiles.

Hardboard: A manufactured pulp board, used as an underlay for resilient tiling.

Jamb: The rebated door frame into which a door closes.

Make good: Return to original, or finish off.

Masonry anchors: Steel bolts with sides which expand in the wall as the bolts are tightened.

MDF board: Medium-density fibreboard – a high-quality manufactured pulp board.

Midway: Usually a shelf for storing knives, food processor blades, or for holding herbs and condiments. It is normally placed midway between the worktop and the wall cupboards, hence the name.

Mineral turpentine (white spirit): A colourless flammable liquid – an essential oil – containing a mixture of terpenes; used as a solvent for paints. Also known as turps.

Mitre joint: A 90° joint between 2 pieces of timber that avoids showing any endgrain by cutting the timber pieces at 45°.

Particleboard: A manufactured wood sheet made of wood chips and adhesive.

Plumb line: Weight attached to a length of string and used to obtain the perpendicular for accurate cupboard fixing.

Polyurethane: A hard yet resilient coating commonly used for wear areas.

PVA adhesive: Water-based glue which is quick drying and clear finishing, used for timber.

Rebate joint: A stepped joint for adding strength to any joint between two pieces of timber.

Scribed joint: A butt joint in which one surface matches the profile of the adjoining one.

Sealer: A coating to provide a suitable surface for final coatings.

Straightedge: A ruler or perfectly straight piece of timber or metal used to give a clean and consistent edge when cutting or trimming.

String line: Any type of string, stretched between two points to mark the line of a wall or path to be built.

Timber studs (wall studs): Vertical wall framing member.

Toggle bolts: Type of bolts for use with hollow walls. Two types are available: spring toggles and gravity toggles. In both cases the toggles open behind the wall lining for fixing.

Underlay: A preparatory surface prior to fixing floor covering.

CONVERSION TABLE

Although most people have some working knowledge of metrics, many cannot visualise the actual size of a metric measurement. Hopefully the following measures will help.

LENGTH
1 mm equals approx $3/64$ in (a paper clip)
10 mm equals approx $3/8$ in (a mortar joint, thickness of the average little finger)
25 mm equals approx 1 in (everyone knows what an inch is!)
230 mm equals approx 9 in (one brick)
820 mm equals approx 32 in (an average door width)
2400 mm equals approx 8 ft (10 bonded bricks, or minimum ceiling height)
1 m equals approx 39 in (a bit higher than a kitchen worktop)
1.8 m equals approx 6 ft (a tall male)
2.04 m equals just under 7 ft (the height of the average door)
3 m equals approx 10 ft (3 ft higher than the average door!)

VOLUME
1 litre equals approx 1.8 pints (a carton of orange juice)
4.5 equals litres approx 1 gallon (a large paint tin)

AREA
1 sq m equals approx 1 sq yd (about 50 bricks laid in a wall)
9.3 sq m equals approx 1 building square – 100 sq ft (an average bedroom)

Index

ACKNOWLEDGMENTS

The Publisher wishes to thank the following for their assistance in the production of this book: E.G. Lefever of James Hardie & Coy Pty Ltd; Dieter Mylius, Advisory Services, Building Centre

Props for front cover: Home & Garden, Skygarden store: Glass canisters (bottom shelf), glass jug and tumblers (middle shelf), patterned bowl (top shelf), sugar bowl, milk jug and glass bottle (window sill)

The Bay Tree, Woollahra: Fruit coffee pot, blue cups and saucers (foreground), green vase, yellow cups and saucers (top shelf), white jug (top shelf), kettle and knife

Cilla Campbell, Australian Floral Designs: White basket and wheat arrangements